教材项目规划小组
Teaching Material Project Planning Group

严美华　姜明宝　王立峰

田小刚　崔邦焱　俞晓敏

赵国成　宋永波　郭　鹏

加拿大方咨询小组
Canadian Consulting Group

Dr. Robert Shanmu Chen

Mr. Zheng Zhining

University of British Columbia

Dr. Helen Wu

University of Toronto

Mr. Wang Renzhong

McGill University

中国国家汉办规划教材

Hanban

NEW PRACTICAL CHINESE READER

(2nd Edition)

1

新实用汉语课本

刘珣 主编

综合练习册
WORKBOOK

英文注释
Annotated in English

编　者：张　凯　刘社会　陈　曦
　　　　左珊丹　施家炜　刘　珣
英译审订：Jerry Schmidt　余心乐

北京语言大学出版社
BEIJING LANGUAGE AND CULTURE
UNIVERSITY PRESS

（第2版）

图书在版编目（CIP）数据

新实用汉语课本综合练习册：英文注释本.1／刘珣主编.
—2版.—北京：北京语言大学出版社，2010.1（2016.7重印）
ISBN 978-7-5619-2622-2

Ⅰ.新…　Ⅱ.刘…　Ⅲ.汉语—对外汉语教学—习题
Ⅳ.H195.4

中国版本图书馆 CIP 数据核字（2010）第 007444 号

书　　名：新实用汉语课本（第2版　英文注释）综合练习册1
中文编辑：王亚莉
英文编辑：侯晓娟
责任印制：汪学发

出版发行：北京语言大学出版社
社　　址：北京市海淀区学院路 15 号　　邮政编码：100083
网　　址：www. blcup. com
电　　话：国内发行　8610-82303650/3591/3648
　　　　　海外发行　8610-82300309/0361/3080/3365
　　　　　编辑部　8610-82303647/3592
　　　　　读者服务部　8610-82303653
　　　　　网上订购电话　8610-82303908
　　　　　客户服务信箱　service@ blcup. com
印　　刷：北京联兴盛业印刷股份有限公司
经　　销：全国新华书店

版　　次：2010 年 1 月第 2 版　2016 年 7 月第 12 次印刷
开　　本：889 毫米×1194 毫米　1/16　印张：9.25
字　　数：129 千字
书　　号：ISBN 978-7-5619-2622-2/H·09312
　　　　　03500

凡有印装质量问题，本社负责调换。电话：8610-82303590
Printed in China

To Our Students

Welcome to the Workbook of *New Practical Chinese Reader (the second edition)*!

New Practical Chinese Reader (the second edition) is a set of Textbooks, Instructor's Manuals, and Workbooks, intended to meet the needs of teachers and students both in and after class. The workbook is provided mainly for *YOU*, the students, to use for after—class practice. It contains exercises on pronunciation, vocabulary, Chinese characters, and grammar. As well, it aims to increase your communicative and linguistic competence in listening, speaking, reading, writing and translating.

These features will facilitate your language learning process:
- Equal emphasis on the fundamental language skills of listening, speaking, reading, and writing;
- Ample exercises to enhance language acquisition and retention;
- A detailed, progressively graded exercise structure;
- Special attention to key points of pronunciation in each lesson.

You will also find this series interesting, timely, and topical; highlighting texts that are current and useful in their Western—Chinese cultural scope.

Remember a last word of advice as you begin:

Practice makes perfect.

第一课
Lesson 1

Nǐ hǎo
你 好
How do you do?

听说练习 Listening and Speaking Exercises

1 听录音，圈出正确的语音。
Circle the right sound according to what you hear on the CD.

1／1~4

1	p	b	l	h
2	m	n	h	l
3	b	n	p	m
4	a	ao	o	uo
5	e	en	ie	in
6	i	ie	in	ing
7	bo	po	huo	luo
8	la	le	li	lü
9	pa	pu	pao	po
10	nie	ni	nin	ning

2 听录音，圈出正确的声调。
Circle the right tone according to what you hear on the CD.

1	ā	á	ǎ	à
2	ī	í	ǐ	ì
3	ēn	én	ěn	èn
4	uō	uó	uǒ	uò
5	hū	hú	hǔ	hù
6	bāo	báo	bǎo	bào

⑦	pīn	pín	pǐn	pìn
⑧	nī	ní	nǐ	nì
⑨	mō	mó	mǒ	mò
⑩	lū	lú	lǔ	lù

3　听录音，为下列音节标出正确的声调。

Mark the right tones on the following syllables according to what you hear on the CD.

① ma　　　　　　　⑥ Lin Na

② li　　　　　　　⑦ hen hao

③ huo　　　　　　⑧ Lu Yuping

④ nin　　　　　　⑨ ni ne

⑤ ye　　　　　　⑩ pa laohu

4　圈出第三声的变调。

Circle the third-tone sandhis.

① A. Ding Libo　　　B. ni hao　　　C. Lin Na

② A. Lu Yuping　　　B. ni ne　　　C. hen hao

5　朗读下列音节和句子。

Read the following syllables and sentences.

①	nā	ná	nǎ	nà
②	hāo	háo	hǎo	hào
③	bō	bó	bǒ	bò
④	līn	lín	lǐn	lìn
⑤		hén	hěn	hèn
⑥	pū	pú	pǔ	pù

⑦ Nǐ hǎo ma?

⑧ Wǒ hěn hǎo.

⑨ Lìbō ne? Lìbō hǎo ma?

⑩ Yě hěn hǎo.

2

6~8

6 听对话，并完成练习。

Listen to the following dialogues and do the exercises.

1 Repeat the dialogues.

2 Answer the questions:

What are they doing? _____

How is the man in the first dialogue doing? _____

In the second dialogue does Lin Na know Libo? _____

How is Lao Li doing in the third dialogue? _____

7 听录音，写拼音。

Listen and write in *pinyin*.

8 角色扮演。

Role-play.

Listen to and imitate the dialogue together with your partner.

9 看图说话。

Say a few sentences according to the picture below.

读写练习　Reading and Writing Exercises

1 按正确的笔顺描汉字，并在后边的空格里写汉字。
Trace over the characters, following the correct stroke order. Then copy the characters in the blank spaces.

一	一	一	一					
八	ノ八	八	八					
力	フ力	力	力					
门	丶冂门	门	门					
也	フ也也	也	也					
马	フ马马	马	马					
女	乀乆女	女	女					
五	一丆五五	五	五					
木	一十才木	木	木					
火	丶丷少火	火	火					

2 在空格里写汉字，注意汉字的部件。
Write the characters in the blank spaces, paying attention to the character components.

lín	木＋木	林						

3　为每个汉字标注拼音，找到相应的图片，并连线。

Give the *pinyin* of the following characters and find the corresponding drawings. Draw a line to connect the two.

（1）木

（2）女

（3）门

（4）火

（5）马

4　用 "ma" 或 "ne" 填空。

Fill in the blanks with "ma" or "ne".

（1）Nǐ hǎo_____?

（2）Wǒ hěn hǎo, nǐ_____?

（3）Lín Nà hǎo_____?

（4）Lín Nà hǎo, Lìbō_____?

5　用汉语拼音翻译下列句子。

Translate the following sentences into Chinese *pinyin*.

（1）How do you do?

_____

（2）How are you?

_____

（3）Fine, and you?

_____

6 不看课本，尽量写出本课出现的汉字。

Write as many characters as you can from this lesson without reading the textbook.

Nǐ máng ma
你 忙 吗
Are you busy?

听说练习 Listening and Speaking Exercises

3
1~4

1 听录音，圈出正确的语音。
Circle the right sound according to what you hear on the CD.

1	b	p	d	t
2	d	t	g	k
3	p	f	h	l
4	e	ei	ie	en
5	o	uo	ou	ao
6	an	ang	en	eng
7	tiao	diao	biao	piao
8	duo	dou	diu	du
9	gao	gan	kao	kan
10	fen	fei	feng	fang

2 听录音，圈出正确的声调。
Circle the right tone according to what you hear on the CD.

1	tān	tán	tǎn	tàn
2	dū	dú	dǔ	dù
3	yōu	yóu	yǒu	yòu
4	fēi	féi	fěi	fèi
5	gēng	géng	gěng	gèng
6	kāng	káng	kǎng	kàng

⑦	liū	liú	liǔ	liù
⑧	piāo	piáo	piǎo	piào
⑨	bēi	béi	běi	bèi
⑩	kān	kán	kǎn	kàn

3 听录音，为下列音节标出正确的声调。

Mark the right tones on the following syllables according to what you hear on the CD.

① ding	⑥ pengyou
② kou	⑦ hen mang
③ teng	⑧ gege
④ bu	⑨ dou yao
⑤ gang	⑩ he kafei

4 圈出轻声，注意：在每一组里可能有不止一个轻声。

Circle the neutral tones; note that in each group, the neutral tone may appear more than once.

①	A. kafei	B. baba	C. pengyou	D. dou hao
②	A. mama	B. hen hao	C. Libo	D. yao he
③	A. ye yao	B. bu mang	C. ni ne	D. tamen
④	A. dou hao	B. hao ma	C. ye mang	D. didi
⑤	A. ni hao	B. ye hao	C. women	D. Yuping

5 朗读下列音节和句子。

Read the following syllables and sentences.

①	yāo	yáo	yǎo	yào
②	nān	nán	nǎn	nàn
③	pēng	péng	pěng	pèng
④	tū	tú	tǔ	tù
⑤	gē	gé	gě	gè
⑥	dī	dí	dǐ	dì

⑦ Bàba、 māma hǎo ma?

Tāmen dōu hěn hǎo.

⑧ Gēge、 dìdi dōu máng ma?

Tāmen dōu bù máng.

⑨ Nǐmen yào kāfēi ma?

Wǒmen dōu hē kāfēi.

6 听对话，并完成练习。

Listen to the following dialogue and do the exercises.

④ 6~9

① Make a similar dialogue.

② Decide whether the statements are true (T) or false (F).

A. Lín Nà hěn máng.　　　　(　　)

B. Tā nán péngyou bù máng.　(　　)

C. Yǔpíng hěn máng.　　　　(　　)

7 听录音，写拼音。

Listen and write in *pinyin*.

8 听录音，写汉字。

Listen and write characters.

9 角色扮演。

Role-play.

Listen to and imitate the dialogue together with your partner.

10 看图说话。
Say a few sentences in Chinese about the picture below.

 读写练习　Reading and Writing Exercises

1 按正确的笔顺描汉字，并在后边的空格里写汉字。
Trace over the characters, following the correct stroke order. Then copy the characters in the blank spaces.

丁	一 丁	丁	丁						
刀	刁 刀	刀	刀						
又	フ 又	叉	叉						
大	一 ナ 大	大	大						
口	丨 冂 口	口	口						
土	一 十 土	土	土						
六	丶 亠 六 六	六	六						
不	一 ア 不 不	不	不						
尼	丆 コ 尸 尸 尼	尼	尼						
可	一 ㄒ 冂 叮 可	可	可						

2 在空格里写汉字，注意汉字的部件。
Write the characters in the blank spaces, paying attention to the character components.

ma	口 + 马	吗					
ne	口 + 尼	呢					
mā	女 + 马	妈					
gē	可 + 可	哥					

3 为下列汉字标注拼音，并在括号里写出笔画数。
Give the *pinyin* of the following characters and write the stroke numbers in the parentheses.

（1）呢 _____ （   ）   （4）哥 _____ （   ）

（2）吗 _____ （   ）   （5）林 _____ （   ）

（3）妈 _____ （   ）

4 为每个汉字标注拼音，找到相应的图片，并连线。
Give the *pinyin* of the following characters and find the corresponding drawings. Draw a line to connect the two.

（1）丁

（2）刀

（3）口

5 用汉语拼音翻译下列句子。

Translate the following sentences into Chinese *pinyin*.

（1）Lin Na is very busy.

_____

（2）He is very busy, too.

_____

（3）Are all of you busy?

_____

（4）Would you like to have some coffee?

_____

6 不看课本，尽量写出本课出现的汉字。

Write as many characters as you can from this lesson without reading the textbook.

Tā shì nǎ guó rén
她 是 哪 国 人
Which country does she come from?

 听说练习 Listening and Speaking Exercises

5
1~4

1 听录音，圈出正确的语音。
Circle the right sound according to what you hear on the CD.

1	zh	ch	sh	r
2	zh	ch	sh	r
3	g	k	sh	r
4	ao	ai	an	uai
5	ang	eng	ong	an
6	iao	iou	uai	ai
7	zhai	chai	shai	chuai
8	zhuai	chuai	shuai	zhai
9	zhong	chong	zhou	chou
10	reng	rang	ri	ren

2 听录音，圈出正确的声调。
Circle the right tone according to what you hear on the CD.

1	zhī	zhí	zhǐ	zhì
2	chuāi	chuái	chuǎi	chuài
3	shēng	shéng	shěng	shèng
4	rāo	ráo	rǎo	rào
5	kāi	kái	kǎi	kài
6	tōng	tóng	tǒng	tòng

⑦	zhān	zhán	zhǎn	zhàn
⑧	chōng	chóng	chǒng	chòng
⑨	shuāi	shuái	shuǎi	shuài
⑩	rū	rú	rǔ	rù

3 听录音，为下列音节标出正确的声调。

Mark the right tones on the following syllables according to what you hear on the CD.

① sheng	⑥ Zhongguo
② zhi	⑦ laoshi
③ che	⑧ yisheng
④ ren	⑨ chifan
⑤ guai	⑩ waiyu ke

4 圈出第三声的变调和"不"的变调。

Circle the third-tone sandhis or tone sandhis of "不".

The third-tone sandhi

① A. yisheng	B. wo shi	C. gege	D. waiyu
② A. ni mang	B. baba	C. zhe shi	D. pengyou
③ A. waipo	B. tamen	C. laoshi	D. Zhongguo

Tone sandhi of "不"

④ A. bu mang	B. bu hao	C. bu shi	D. bu he
⑤ A. bu hao	B. bu he	C. bu dou	D. bu yao

5 朗读下列音节和句子。

Read the following syllables and sentences.

① chā	chá	chǎ	chà
② zhē	zhé	zhě	zhè
③ shū	shú	shǔ	shù
④	rú	rǔ	rù
⑤ chōng	chóng	chǒng	chòng

6 guāi　　　　　　　　guǎi　　　　guài

7 Gēge：Nà shì shéi?

　　Dìdi：Nà shì wǒmen lǎoshī.

　　Gēge：Nǐmen lǎoshī shì nǎ guó rén?

　　Dìdi：Tā shì Zhōngguó rén.

8 Zhè shì wǒ nán péngyou. Tā bú shì wàiyǔ lǎoshī, tā shì yīshēng.

6 听对话，并完成练习。

Listen to the following dialogue and do the exercises.

1 Make a similar dialogue.

2 Decide whether the statements are true (T) or false (F).

　　A. Chén lǎoshī shì yīshēng.　　　　　　（　　）

　　B. Dīng Lìbō de gēge shì lǎoshī.　　　　（　　）

　　C. Chén lǎoshī shì Zhōngguó rén.　　　（　　）

7 听录音，写拼音。

Listen and write in *pinyin*.

8 听录音，写汉字。

Listen and write characters.

9 角色扮演。

Role-play.

Listen to and imitate the dialogue together with your partner.

读写练习　*Reading and Writing Exercises*

1 按正确的笔顺描汉字，并在后边的空格里写汉字。

Trace over the characters, following the correct stroke order. Then copy the characters in the blank spaces.

人	丿人	人	人					
十	一十	十	十					
匕	丿匕	匕	匕					
中	丨冂口中	中	中					
日	丨冂月日	日	日					
贝	丨冂贝贝	贝	贝					
玉	一二干王玉	玉	玉					
矢	丿仁二午矢	矢	矢					
生	丿仁二牛生	生	生					
者	一十土耂者者者	者	者					

2 在空格里写汉字，注意汉字的部件。

Write the characters in the blank spaces, paying attention to the character components.

tā	女 + 也	她						
tā	亻 + 也	他						
men	亻 + 门	们						

nǐ	亻 + 尔	你								
nà	月 + 阝	那								
nǎ	口 + 那	哪								
nà	女 + 那	娜								
dōu	者 + 阝	都								
lǎo	少 + 匕	老								
shī	丿 + 帀	师								
guó	囗 + 玉	国								
yī	匚 + 矢	医								
shì	日 + 疋	是								

3 为下列汉字标注拼音，并在括号里写出笔画数。

Give the *pinyin* of the following characters and write the stroke numbers in the parentheses.

（1）哪 _____ （　　） 　　（4）师 _____ （　　）

（2）国 _____ （　　） 　　（5）医 _____ （　　）

（3）老 _____ （　　） 　　（6）生 _____ （　　）

4 根据所给拼音，在第二行中找到能与第一行汉字组成词语的汉字，并连线。

Find a character in the second line which can be combined with a character in the first line to make a word according to the *pinyin* provided. Draw a line to connect the two.

（1）wàiyǔ　　（2）lǎoshī　　（3）yīshēng　　（4）Zhōngguó　　（5）tāmen

他　　　　老　　　　中　　　　医　　　　外

生　　　　们　　　　语　　　　国　　　　师

5 为下列句子标注拼音，并译成英文。

Write the *pinyin* of the following sentences and then translate the sentences into English.

（1）谁是陈老师？

_____?

_____?

（2）他哥哥是医生吗？

_____?

_____?

（3）您是哪国人？

_____?

_____?

（4）他是中国人。

_____.

_____.

6 连接Ⅰ和Ⅱ两部分的词语，组成句子。

Make sentences by matching words from part Ⅰ with those from part Ⅱ. Draw a line to connect them.

Ⅰ

那是

林娜

陈老师是

Ⅱ

是我朋友

谁

中国人

7 用汉语拼音翻译下列句子。

Translate the following sentences into Chinese *pinyin*.

（1）Our teacher is Chinese.

_____

（2）She is my friend.

_____

（3）He is my boyfriend.

_____

（4）Who is he?

_____

8 不看课本，尽量写出本课出现的汉字。

Write as many characters as you can from this lesson without reading the textbook.

9 看图写句子。

Write a few sentences in Chinese about the pictures below.

A Summary of Personal Pronouns

Singular		Plural	
我 wǒ		我们 wǒmen	
你 nǐ	您 nín	你们 nǐmen	
他 tā	她 tā	他们 tāmen	她们 tāmen

Rènshi nǐ hěn gāoxìng
认识 你 很 高兴
Nice to meet you!

听说练习 Listening and Speaking Exercises

7
1~4

1 听录音，圈出正确的语音。
Circle the right sound according to what you hear on the CD.

1	j	q	zh	ch
2	q	sh	x	r
3	j	zh	x	q
4	ia	iao	ian	iang
5	uai	uei	uen	en
6	ü	üe	yi	ie
7	jia	qia	jian	qian
8	que	xue	quan	xuan
9	zhui	chui	zhun	chun
10	chao	xiao	qiang	jie

2 听录音，圈出正确的声调。
Circle the right tone according to what you hear on the CD.

1	jiā	jiá	jiǎ	jià
2	qiān	qián	qiǎn	qiàn
3	xiāng	xiáng	xiǎng	xiàng
4	juē	jué	juě	juè
5	xuān	xuán	xuǎn	xuàn
6	qiē	qié	qiě	qiè

⑦	shuī	shuí	shuǐ	shuì
⑧	chūn	chún	chǔn	chùn
⑨	zhōng	zhóng	zhǒng	zhòng
⑩	rēn	rén	rěn	rèn

3 听录音，为下列音节标出正确的声调。

Mark the right tones on the following syllables according to what you hear on the CD.

① xiao   ⑥ guixing

② shei   ⑦ yuyan

③ jian   ⑧ renshi

④ qi   ⑨ jiao Lin Na

⑤ xing   ⑩ xuexi Hanyu

4 圈出第三声的变调，注意：每一组里第三声的变调可能不止出现一次。

Circle the third-tone sandhis; note that in each group, the third-tone sandhi may appear more than once.

① A. ta hao   B. ni hao   C. wo hao   D. dou hao

② A. qing jin   B. nin qing   C. qingwen   D. jinlai

③ A. xuesheng   B. yisheng   C. jizhe   D. laoshi

④ A. xueyuan   B. yuyan   C. xuexi   D. keyi

⑤ A. Zhongguo   B. Yingguo   C. Meiguo   D. Jianada

5 朗读下列音节和句子。

Read the following syllables and sentences.

①	jīn		jǐn	jìn
②	qiā	qiá	qiǎ	qià
③	xiān	xián	xiǎn	xiàn
④	juān		juǎn	juàn
⑤	qiāng	qiáng	qiǎng	qiàng
⑥	xuē	xué	xuě	xuè

7　Lín Nà, wǒ kěyǐ jìnlai ma?

Qǐng jìn, Yáng lǎoshī.

8　Qǐngwèn, nín guìxìng?

Wǒ xìng Mǎ,　jiào Mǎ Dàwéi. Wǒ shì Měiguó rén, shì Yǔyán Xuéyuàn de

xuésheng.

Wǒ xuéxí Hànyǔ. Rènshi nǐ hěn gāoxìng.

6　听对话，并完成练习。

8　Listen to the following dialogue and do the exercises.
6~9

① Choose the right answer:

Under what circumstances does one use the expression "请进"？（　　）

A. The speaker is in the room.

B. The speaker is outside the room.

C. A polite way of inviting guests to enter a room.

② Decide whether the statements are true (T) or false (F).

A. Lù Yǔpíng shì yīshēng.　（　　）

B. Lù Yǔpíng shì jìzhě.　（　　）

C. Jìzhě xìng Yǔpíng.　（　　）

7　听录音，写拼音。

Listen and write in *pinyin*.

8　听录音，写汉字。

Listen and write characters.

9 角色扮演。
Role-play.

Listen to and imitate the dialogue together with your partner.

读写练习　Reading and Writing Exercises

1 按正确的笔顺描汉字，并在后边的空格里写汉字。
Trace over the characters, following the correct stroke order. Then copy the characters in the blank spaces.

七	一七	七	七				
小	亅小小	小	小				
心	心心心心	心	心				
水	亅水水水	水	水				
月	丿月月月	月	月				
手	一二三手	手	手				
田	丨冂日田田	田	田				
白	丿白白白白	白	白				
只	丨冂口只只	只	只				
言	丶一二言言言言	言	言				

2 在空格里写汉字，注意汉字的部件。

Write the characters in the blank spaces, paying attention to the character components.

rèn	讠＋人	认					
shí	讠＋只	识					
hàn	氵＋又	汉					
yǔ	讠＋五＋口	语					
nín	你＋心	您					
péng	月＋月	朋					
yǒu	ナ＋又	友					
guì	中＋一＋贝	贵					
xìng	女＋生	姓					
jiào	口＋丩	叫					
de	白＋勺	的					

3 为下列汉字标注拼音，并在括号里写出笔画数。

Give the *pinyin* of the following characters and write the stroke numbers in the parentheses.

（1）识 _____ （　　　） 　　（4）您 _____ （　　　）

（2）语 _____ （　　　） 　　（5）贵 _____ （　　　）

（3）水 _____ （　　　）

4 根据所给拼音，在第二行中找到能与第一行汉字组成词语的汉字，并连线。

Find a character in the second line which can be combined with a character in the first line to make a word according to the *pinyin* provided. Draw a line to connect the two.

（1）Hànyǔ　　（2）péngyou　　（3）guìxìng　　（4）rènshi　　（5）xuésheng

学　　　　朋　　　　汉　　　　贵　　　　认

识　　　　姓　　　　生　　　　友　　　　语

5 为下列句子标注拼音，并译成英文。

Write the *pinyin* of the following sentences and then translate the sentences into English.

（1）您认识语言学院的杨老师吗？

_____?

_____?

（2）马大为学习汉语。

_____.

_____.

（3）请问，您贵姓？

_____?

_____?

（4）认识您，我很高兴。

_____.

_____.

6 填空。

Fill in the blanks.

（1）丁力波学习_____。

（2）您_____？

（3）_____你很高兴。

（4）我_____林，_____林娜。

7 用汉语拼音翻译下列句子。
Translate the following sentences into Chinese *pinyin*.

（1）I study Chinese.

_____.

（2）Nice to meet you！

_____.

（3）May I have your surname?

_____?

（4）May I come in?

_____?

8 不看课本，尽量写出本课出现的汉字。
Write as many characters as you can from this lesson without reading the textbook.

9 看图写句子。
Write a few sentences in Chinese about the picture below.

A Summary of Third-tone Sandhi

(1) When a third-tone syllable appears alone or at the end of a word, it is pronounced in original third tone. For example:

      hǎo   qǐng   gěi

      túshūguǎn

(2) Third tone + third tone → second tone + third tone. For example:

      nǐ　+ hǎo → ní　+ hǎo

      wǒ + mǎi → wó + mǎi

(3) Third tone + non-third tone → half third tone + non-third tone. For example:

      Qǐng hē kāfēi.

      Nǐ máng ma?

      Qǐng jìn !

      Nǐ ne?

      Hǎo ma?

(4) When three third tones appear in series with no pauses in between, the first two are pronounced in the second tone. For example:

      zhǎnlǎnguǎn　→ zhánlánguǎn

      Wǒ hěn hǎo. → Wó hén hǎo.

Cāntīng zài nǎr

餐厅 在 哪儿

Where is the dining hall?

 听说练习 Listening and Speaking Exercises

9
1~4

1 听录音，圈出正确的语音。
Circle the right sound according to what you hear on the CD.

1	z	c	zh	ch
2	c	ch	s	sh
3	zh	sh	s	z
4	e	er	en	ei
5	ua	uan	iang	uang
6	ün	un	ong	iong
7	zi	ci	zhi	chi
8	suan	zuan	shuan	zhuan
9	cai	chai	sai	shai
10	jun	jiong	zhuan	zhuang

2 听录音，圈出正确的声调。
Circle the right tone according to what you hear on the CD.

1	sān	sán	sǎn	sàn
2	cī	cí	cǐ	cì
3	zuān	zuán	zuǎn	zuàn
4	ēr	ér	ěr	èr
5	xiōng	xióng	xiǒng	xiòng
6	guā	guá	guǎ	guà

⑦	kuāng	kuáng	kuǎng	kuàng
⑧	jūn	jún	jǔn	jùn
⑨	cēng	céng	cěng	cèng
⑩	zāi	zái	zǎi	zài

3 听录音，为下列音节标出正确的声调。

Mark the right tones on the following syllables according to what you hear on the CD.

① qing　　　　　　　　⑥ qing jin

② zi　　　　　　　　　⑦ zaijian

③ er　　　　　　　　　⑧ xiaojie

④ si　　　　　　　　　⑨ canting

⑤ zuo　　　　　　　　⑩　Wang Xiaoyun

4 圈出儿化韵。

Circle the retroflex endings.

① A. wan le　　B. guanxi　　C. nar　　D. si ceng

② A. zhe shi　　B. zher　　C. zhidao　　D. zai ma

5 朗读下列音节和句子。

Read the following syllables and sentences.

①	cān	cán	cǎn	càn
②	sāng		sǎng	sàng
③	zuō	zuó	zuǒ	zuò
④	yūn	yún	yǔn	yùn
⑤	wān	wán	wǎn	wàn
⑥	wāng	wáng	wǎng	wàng

⑦ Zhè shì Wáng Xiǎoyún de sùshè. Qǐng jìn, qǐng zuò. Wáng Xiǎoyún bú zài

sùshè. Tā zài nǎr? Duìbuqǐ, wǒ bù zhīdào. Búyòng xiè. Méi guānxi. Zàijiàn.

⑧ Wáng Xiǎoyún、Sòng Huá zài cāntīng, tāmen zài èr céng sì líng èr hào.

⑨ Mǎ Dàwéi lái wǎn le.

6 听对话，并完成练习。

Listen to the following dialogue and do the exercises.

① Choose the correct answer:

Where is Wang Xiaoyun's dorm?　（　　）

    A. 在二层四〇二

    B. 在二层二〇四

    C. 在四层二〇四

② Decide whether the statements are true (T) or false (F).

    A. 王小云在宿舍。　　　　　　　　（　　）

    B. 男士（nánshì，the man）在二层二〇四。　（　　）

    C. 男士在宿舍。　　　　　　　　　（　　）

7 听录音，写拼音。

Listen and write in *pinyin*.

8 听录音，写汉字。

Listen and write characters.

9 角色扮演。

Role-play.

Listen to and imitate the dialogue together with your partner.

读写练习　Reading and Writing Exercises

1 按正确的笔顺描汉字，并在后边的空格里写汉字。

Trace over the characters, following the correct stroke order. Then copy the characters in the blank spaces.

二	一 二	二	二						
儿	丿 儿	儿	儿						
子	乛 了 子	子	子						
井	一 二 井 井	井	井						
文	丶 一 ナ 文	文	文						
见	丨 冂 贝 见	见	见						
且	丨 冂 月 月 且	且	且						
四	丨 冂 叼 四 四	四	四						
我	一 二 于 于 我 我 我	我	我						
青	一 二 丰 丰 青 青 青	青	青						

2 在空格里写汉字，注意汉字的部件。

Write the characters in the blank spaces, paying attention to the character components.

zuò	人 + 人 + 土	坐						
zài	才 + 土	在						
qǐng	讠 + 青	请						
wèn	门 + 口	问						

zhè	文 + 辶	这						
jìn	井 + 辶	进						
zài	一 + 冂 + 土	再						
xué	𭕄 + 子	学						
hǎo	女 + 子	好						
jiě	女 + 且	姐						
yòng	冂 + 丯	用						

3 为下列汉字标注拼音，并在括号里写出笔画数。

Give the *pinyin* of the following characters and write the stroke numbers in the parentheses.

（1）坐 ＿＿＿＿＿（　　　）　　　（4）学 ＿＿＿＿＿（　　　）

（2）谢 ＿＿＿＿＿（　　　）　　　（5）姐 ＿＿＿＿＿（　　　）

（3）请 ＿＿＿＿＿（　　　）

4 根据所给拼音，在第二行中找到能与第一行汉字组成词语的汉字，并连线。

Find a character in the second line which can be combined with a character in the first line to make a word according to the *pinyin* provided. Draw a line to connect the two.

（1）zàijiàn　　（2）qǐngwèn　　（3）xiǎojie　　（4）cāntīng　　（5）zhīdao

请　　　再　　　小　　　知　　　餐

厅　　　姐　　　问　　　见　　　道

5 为下列句子标注拼音，并译成英文。

Write the *pinyin* of the following sentences and then translate the sentences into English.

（1）请问，学生餐厅在哪儿？

_____？

_____？

（2）对不起，我不知道。

_____．

_____．

（3）他的宿舍在三层。

_____．

_____．

（4）小姐，你认识王小云吗？

_____？

_____？

（5）对不起，我来晚了。

_____．

_____．

6 用恰当的汉字填空。

Fill in the blanks with proper characters.

（1）林娜不_____宿舍。

（2）请_____，请_____。

（3）餐厅_____哪儿？

（4）对不起，_____来晚了。

7 用所给词语造句。

Write sentences with the words given.

（1）宿舍　我　在

_____

（2）哪儿 在 餐厅

_____

（3）他 在 不

_____

（4）知道 你 吗

_____

8 把下列句子译成中文。

Translate the following sentences into Chinese.

（1）Where are you?

_____?

（2）I am here.

_____.

（3）I know Miss Wang.

_____.

（4）May I ask where she is?

_____?

9 不看课本，尽量写出本课出现的汉字。

Write as many characters as you can from this lesson without reading the textbook.

10 看图写句子，注意用上"……在哪儿"。

Write a few sentences in Chinese using "……在哪儿" according to the picture below.

A Summary of Spelling Rules

(1) i and y

i ⇨ y

examples: ia → ya　　　ie → ye　　　ian → yan　　　iang → yang

iao → yao　　　iou → you　　　iong → yong

i ⇨ yi

Examples: i → yi　　　in → yin　　　ing → ying

(2) u and w

u ⇨ w

Examples: ua → wa　　　　uan → wan

uo → wo　　　　uen → wen

uai → wai　　　uang → wang

uei → wei　　　ueng → weng

u ⇨ wu

Examples: u → wu

(3) ü and y

ü ⇨ yu

Examples: ü → yu　　　üe → yue　　　üan → yuan　　　ün → yun

ü and initials n, l:

l + ü → lü　　　　example:　　lǜ 绿 (green)

n + ü → nü　　　　example:　　nǚ 女 (female)

(4) -iu, -ui, -un

Initial + {iou / uei / uen} → Initial + {iu / ui / un}　　example: {píjiǔ 啤酒(beer) / guìxìng 贵姓 / tǎolùn 讨论 (to discuss)}

(5) The position of tone marks

The tone marks are placed on vowels in the sequence "a-o-e-i-u-ü".
For example:

Wáng xiānsheng hěn hǎo.

Wǒmen dōu hěn máng.

Nín shì Jiānádà liúxuéshēng ma?

The finals iou and uei are simplified to -iu and -ui when they are combined with initials. Tone marks required by these two finals are placed over the last vowel. For example: liù (六)，guìxìng (贵姓).

(6) Syllable-dividing marks "'"

Examples: Tiān'ān Mén 天安门 (Tian'anmen)

Xī'ōu 西欧 (Western Europe)

Wǒmen qù yóuyǒng, hǎo ma
我们 去 游泳， 好 吗

Let's go swimming, shall we?

（复习 Review）

听说练习 Listening and Speaking Exercises

11
1~4

1 听录音，圈出正确的语音。

Circle the right sound according to what you hear on the CD.

1	b	p	d	t	g	k
2	z	c	zh	ch	j	q
3	f	h	s	sh	x	r
4	c	x	j	z	s	q
5	an	ian	ao	iao	ai	uai
6	ün	uen	in	ing	ong	iong
7	pei	bei	kei	dei		
8	zao	sao	jiao	xiao		
9	shen	zhen	sheng	zheng		
10	bo	duo	po	tuo		
11	xiong	qing	xiang	jing		
12	gou	duo	kou	tuo		

2 听录音，圈出正确的声调。

Circle the right tone according to what you hear on the CD.

1	cūn	cún	cǔn	cùn
2	sī	sí	sǐ	sì
3	jiū	jiú	jiǔ	jiù
4	gōng	góng	gǒng	gòng

⑤ yū	yú	yǔ	yù
⑥ qīng	qíng	qǐng	qìng
⑦ pāo	páo	pǎo	pào
⑧ xiōng	xióng	xiǒng	xiòng
⑨ dōu	dóu	dǒu	dòu
⑩ zuō	zuó	zuǒ	zuò

3 听录音，为下列音节标出正确的声调。

Mark the right tones on the following syllables according to what you hear on the CD.

① dui   ⑥ xianzai

② jiu   ⑦ shijian

③ xi   ⑧ tai mang

④ lao   ⑨ you yisi

⑤ peng   ⑩ mingtian qu

4 圈出"一"的变调，注意：每一组里"一"的变调可能不止出现一次。

Circle the tone sandhis of "一"; note that in each group, the tone sandhi of "一" may appear more than once.

① A. yi   B. yi biàn   C. yi tiān   D. wéiyi

② A. yi, èr   B. yi běn   C. dì yi   D. yizhí

5 朗读下列音节和句子。

Read the following syllables and sentences.

① xiān	xián	xiǎn	xiàn
② jū	jú	jǔ	jù
③ qiāng	qiáng	qiǎng	qiàng
④ zuō	zuó	zuǒ	zuò
⑤ bāo	báo	bǎo	bào
⑥	míng	mǐng	mìng

⑦ Zuótiān de jīngjù hěn yǒu yìsi. Wǒ hěn gāoxìng.

Jīntiān tiānqì hěn hǎo, wǒmen qù yóuyǒng, hǎo ma?

Tài hǎo le!

Wǒmen xiànzài qù, kěyǐ ma? Nǐ yǒu shíjiān ma? Nǐ hěn máng, kǒngpà bù

xíng? Méi guānxi. Wǒmen míngtiān qù.

6 朗读下列音节，注意你的发音。

Practice the following syllables, paying attention to your pronunciation.

① 声调　The tones

Zhōngguó	中国	huǒtuǐcháng	火腿肠
Měiguó	美国	Màidāngláo	麦当劳
Éluósī	俄罗斯	Kěndéjī	肯德基
Rìběn	日本	yóuyǒng	游泳
Zhōngwén	中文	qíchē	骑车
Fǎwén	法文	huáxuě	滑雪
Déwén	德文	dǎ qiú	打球
Rìwén	日文	tī zúqiú	踢足球
Yīngyǔ	英语	dǎ lánqiú	打篮球
Fǎyǔ	法语	dǎ wǎngqiú	打网球
Déyǔ	德语	dǎ páiqiú	打排球
Hànyǔ	汉语	gǎnlǎnqiú	橄榄球
hànbǎo	汉堡	qūgùnqiú	曲棍球
huángyóu	黄油	chōnglàng	冲浪
miànbāo	面包	jiànshēn	健身
nǎilào	奶酪	dēngshān	登山
sānmíngzhì	三明治	yùndòng	运动

② 轻声　The neutral tone

shūshu	叔叔	qīzi	妻子
mǔqin	母亲	jiějie	姐姐
yéye	爷爷	xiānsheng	先生
xiōngdi	兄弟	qīnqi	亲戚
péngyou	朋友	rénjia	人家

xuésheng	学生	hòubianr	后边儿
kèren	客人	nǎge	哪个
biéren	别人	qīngchu	清楚
yìsi	意思	piàoliang	漂亮
shíhou	时候	máfan	麻烦
mùtou	木头	shúxi	熟悉
yīfu	衣服	xièxie	谢谢
bùfen	部分	juéde	觉得
wěiba	尾巴	xǐhuan	喜欢
bèizi	被子	xiàohua	笑话

3 儿化韵 The retroflex ending

dōngbianr	东边儿	xiàbianr	下边儿
nánbianr	南边儿	lǐbianr	里边儿
xībianr	西边儿	wàibianr	外边儿
běibianr	北边儿	zuǒbianr	左边儿
qiánbianr	前边儿	yòubianr	右边儿
hòubianr	后边儿	pángbiānr	旁边儿
shàngbianr	上边儿	duìmiànr	对面儿

12
7~10

7 听对话，并完成练习。
Listen to the following dialogue and do the exercises.

1 Choose the correct answers.

他们现在去游泳吗？（   ）

A. 他们现在去。

B. 他们明天去。

C. 他们今天去。

明天天气好吗？（   ）

A. 明天天气不好。

B. 明天天气很好。

C. 今天天气很好。

2 Decide whether the statements are true (T) or false (F).

A. 马大为明天游泳。 （ ）

B. 宋华现在不忙。 （ ）

C. 马大为明天很忙。 （ ）

D. 他们明天游泳。 （ ）

8 听录音，写拼音。
Listen and write in *pinyin*.

9 听录音，写汉字。
Listen and write characters.

10 角色扮演。
Role-play.

Listen to and imitate the dialogue together with your partner.

 读写练习 Reading and Writing Exercises

1 按正确的笔顺描汉字，并在后边的空格里写汉字。

Trace over the characters, following the correct stroke order. Then copy the characters in the blank spaces.

九	丿九	九	九					
厶	厶厶	厶	厶					

寸	一 十 寸	寸	寸						
工	一 丁 工	工	工						
亡	、 亠 亡	亡	亡						
三	一 二 三	三	三						
气	丿 一 气 气	气	气						
立	、 亠 六 立 立	立	立						
身	丿 亻 亇 自 身 身 身	身	身						
兑	、 丷 丷 兯 兯 兑 兑	兑	兑						

2 在空格里写汉字，注意汉字的部件。
Write the characters in the blank spaces, paying attention to the character components.

qù	土 + 厶	去							
yǒu	𠂇 + 月	有							
yì	立 + 日 + 心	意							
sī	田 + 心	思							
tiān	一 + 大	天							
tài	大 + 丶	太							
shén	亻 + 十	什							
me	丿 + 厶	么							
shí	日 + 寸	时							

hòu	亻 + 丨 + 二 + 矢	候							
xiàn	王 + 见	现							
míng	日 + 月	明							
jiān	门 + 日	间							
shuō	讠 + 兑	说							
máng	忄 + 亡	忙							
xiè	讠 + 身 + 寸	谢							

3 选择恰当的汉字填空。

Fill in the blanks with proper characters.

（1）林娜不_____宿舍。

　　A. 再　　　　　　B. 在　　　　　　C. 坐

（2）这是他朋_____。

　　A. 友　　　　　　B. 有　　　　　　C. 又

（3）_____是他们的外语老师？

　　A. 识　　　　　　B. 认　　　　　　C. 谁

（4）他很忙，我不_____忙。

　　A. 大　　　　　　B. 太　　　　　　C. 天

4 根据所给拼音，在第二行中找到能与第一行汉字组成词语的汉字，并连线。

Find a character in the second line which can be combined with a character in the first line to make a word according to the *pinyin* provided. Draw a line to connect the two.

（1）míngtiān　　（2）yóuyǒng　　（3）shíjiān　　（4）xiànzài　　（5）jīngjù

京　　　时　　　明　　　游　　　现

天　　　在　　　剧　　　间　　　泳

5 为下列句子标注拼音，并译成英文。

Write the *pinyin* of the following sentences and then translate the sentences into English.

（1）我们去游泳。

_____.

_____.

（2）明天天气怎么样?

_____?

_____?

（3）张老师很忙。

_____.

_____.

（4）京剧很有意思。

_____.

_____.

（5）很抱歉，我现在没有时间。

_____.

_____.

6 填空。

Fill in the blanks.

（1）林娜有_____游泳。

（2）昨天的京剧很_____。

（3）今天_____很好。

（4）对不起，我很_____。

7 用所给词语造句。

Write sentences with the words given.

（1）今天 时间 我 有

_____

（2）谢　用　不

_____

（3）时候　我们　去　什么

_____

（4）很　他　忙

_____

8 用汉语拼音翻译下列句子。

Translate the following sentences into Chinese *pinyin*.

（1）It is a nice day today.

_____

（2）It is wonderful.

_____

（3）It is very interesting.

_____

（4）I am afraid that I cannot go swimming now.

_____

9 不看课本，尽量写出本课出现的汉字。

Write as many characters as you can from this lesson without reading the textbook.

10 看图写句子。

Write a few sentences in Chinese about the picture below.

Grammar Summary

We have studied:

	Affirmative statement	Yes-no question	Negative statement	Question-word question
Sentences with an adjectival predicate	你好！ Nǐ hǎo!	你忙吗？ Nǐ máng ma?	我不忙。 Wǒ bù máng.	京剧怎么样？ Jīngjù zěnme-yàng?
Sentences with "是"	这是我朋友。 Zhè shì wǒ péngyou.	他也是老师吗？ Tā yě shì lǎoshī ma?	他不是老师。 Tā bú shì lǎoshī.	那是谁？ Nà shì shéi?
Sentences with a verbal predicate	我学习汉语。 Wǒ xuéxí Hànyǔ.	宋华在家吗？ Sòng Huá zài jiā ma?	他不要咖啡。 Tā bú yào kāfēi.	你姓什么？ Nǐ xìng shénme?

听说练习 Listening and Speaking Exercises

1 发音练习。
Pronunciation drills.

1 Read the following words or phrases, paying attention to the tone sandhis of "一".

yī	一	dì yī kè	第一课
shíyī lóu	十一楼	dì yī tí	第一题
yízhì	一致	yìxiē	一些
yìshēng	一生	yìbān	一般
yìbiān	一边	yìqí	一齐
yìzhí	一直	yìqǐ	一起
yíbàn	一半	yídìng	一定
yígòng	一共	yíqiè	一切
yíyàng	一样		

2 Read the following words or sentences aloud, paying special attention to the pronunciation of "j, q, x" and word stress.

介绍	教授	请问	请进	请坐	加拿大
学生	学院	学习	贵姓	谢谢	开学

qìxiàngzhàn（气象站）

wén jī qǐ wǔ（闻鸡起舞）

jí zhōng shēng zhì（急中生智）

Qīng zhōu yǐ guò wàn chóng shān.（轻舟已过万重山。）

2 听问题，并圈出正确的回答。
Listen to each question and circle the correct answer.

① A. 忙　　　B. 不是忙　　　C. 不是　　　D. 是很忙

② A. 我介绍　　B. 认识　　　C. 在哪儿　　D. 学生

③ A. 是　　　B. 学生　　　C. 他们　　　D. 老师

④ A. 我说汉语　B. 我听汉语　　C. 我学习汉语　D. 我学习英语

⑤ A. 是教授　　B. 认识他　　C. 不是老师　　D. 他很忙

⑥ A. 英语专业　B. 美术专业　　C. 汉语专业　　D. 文学专业

3 听对话，并判断正误。
Listen to the following dialogue and decide whether the statements are true (T) or false (F).

① 她很忙。（　　　）

② 他不忙。（　　　）

4 听录音，并填空。
Listen and fill in the blanks.

① 我学习_____。

② 我_____一下。

③ 他学习_____专业。

④ 他是_____老师。

5 听录音，写汉字。
Listen and write characters.

6 角色扮演。
Role-play.

Listen to and imitate the dialogue together with your partner.

读写练习　Reading and Writing Exercises

1 按正确的笔顺描汉字，并在后边的空格里写汉字。

Trace over the characters, following the correct stroke order. Then copy the characters in the blank spaces.

开	一 二 开 开	开	开					
父	丿 八 父 父	父	父					
巴	丁 刀 口 巴	巴	巴					
习	丁 习 习	习	习					
专	一 二 专 专	专	专					
业	丨 刂 刂 业 业	业	业					
羊	丶 丷 二 兰 羊	羊	羊					
术	一 十 才 木 术	术	术					
系	丿 乙 至 至 至 至 系	系	系					
皮	一 厂 广 皮 皮	皮	皮					
为	丶 丿 为 为	为	为					
目	丨 冂 月 目 目	目	目					
介	丿 人 介 介	介	介					
下	一 丁 下	下	下					
元	一 二 亓 元	元	元					
片	丿 丿 广 片	片	片					

弓	ㄱㄱ弓	弓	弓					
长	ノ亡长长	长	长					
来	一丷丌业来来来	来	来					

2 在空格里写汉字，注意汉字的部件。

Write the characters in the blank spaces, paying attention to the character components.

shéi	讠+隹	谁						
shào	纟+刀+口	绍						
míng	夕+口	名						
zì	宀+子	字						
bà	父+巴	爸						
měi	羊+大	美						
bō	氵+皮	波						
jiā	力+口	加						
ná	人+冖+口+手	拿						
kàn	手+目	看						
yuàn	阝+宀+元	院						
à	口+阝+可	啊						
jiào	耂+子+攵	教						
shòu	扌+龸+冖+又	授						

hěn	彳 + 艮	很						
gāo	亠 + 口 + 冂 + 口	高						
xìng	丷 + 一 + 八	兴						
zhāng	弓 + 长	张						

3 为下列汉字标注拼音，并把它们分解为部件。

Write *pinyin* for the following characters and devide them into character components.

E. g. 剧 jù → 尸 + 古 + 刂

（1）姓　　　　　　　　（6）请

（2）语　　　　　　　　（7）妈

（3）师　　　　　　　　（8）那

（4）汉　　　　　　　　（9）都

（5）们　　　　　　　　（10）的

4 根据所给拼音，在第二行中找到能与第一行汉字组成词语的汉字，并连线。

Find a character in the second line which can be combined with a character in the first line to make a word according to the *pinyin* provided. Draw a line to connect the two.

（1）kāixué　　（2）xìngmíng　　（3）zhuānyè　　（4）yīyuàn　　（5）Zhōngguó

医　　　　　姓　　　　　专　　　　　开　　　　　中

名　　　　　业　　　　　院　　　　　国　　　　　学

5 为下列句子标注拼音，并译成英文。

Write the *pinyin* of the following sentences and then translate the sentences into English.

（1）马大为是美国人。

_____.

_____.

（2）张先生是语言学院的教授。

_____.

_____.

（3）您认识不认识林娜?

_____?

_____?

（4）谁是你们的汉语老师?

_____?

_____?

（5）丁力波是不是加拿大人?

_____?

_____?

6 猜字谜。_____
Character riddle.

人有"他"大，

天没"他"大。

请问"他"是谁?

你也认识"他"。

（The key is a character.）

7 完成下列对话。_____
Complete the following dialogues.

（1）A: _____?

B: 他是张教授。

（2）A: _____?

B: 他学习汉语。

（3）A: _____?

B: 我很忙。

（4）A: _____?

B: 我叫林娜。

（5）A: _____?

B: 我是加拿大人。

8 连接Ⅰ和Ⅱ两部分的词语，组成句子。

Make sentences by matching words from part Ⅰ with those from part Ⅱ. Draw a line to connect them.

Ⅰ	Ⅱ
他学习	我的老师
张教授是	汉语
我来介绍	学生
林娜是	一个哥哥
我有	一下

9 把下列陈述句变为疑问句。

Change the following statements into questions.

E.g. 我是学生。→你是学生吗？

（1）我学习汉语。→ _____?

（2）我学习美术专业。→ _____?

（3）我很忙。→ _____?

（4）他不认识我。→ _____?

（5）我是加拿大人。→ _____?

（6）我们都认识他。→ _____?

10 用所给词语造句。

Make sentences with the words given.

认识：＿＿＿＿＿＿＿＿＿＿＿＿＿＿＿＿＿

都：＿＿＿＿＿＿＿＿＿＿＿＿＿＿＿＿＿

也：＿＿＿＿＿＿＿＿＿＿＿＿＿＿＿＿＿

一下：＿＿＿＿＿＿＿＿＿＿＿＿＿＿＿＿

11 根据本课课文判断正误。

Decide whether the statements are true (T) or false (F) according to the text of this lesson.

（1）林娜明天开学。　　　　　　（　　）

（2）张教授不是语言学院的老师。（　　）

（3）张教授不忙。　　　　　　　（　　）

（4）马大为是加拿大人。　　　　（　　）

（5）丁力波是林娜的朋友。　　　（　　）

（6）丁力波学习语言专业。　　　（　　）

12 选择正确的答案。

Choose the correct answers.

（1）你在＿＿＿＿＿＿工作？

　　A. 哪儿　　　　B. 我　　　　C. 医生　　　　D. 谁

（2）A：你是老师吗？

　　B：＿＿＿＿＿＿。

　　A. 你　　　　B. 老师　　　　C. 我　　　　D. 不是

（3）A：你贵姓？

　　B：＿＿＿＿＿＿。

　　A. 我是学生　　B. 我姓王　　　C. 我很忙　　　D. 我很好

13 写一段话描述下列图片。
Write a short paragraph describing the pictures below.

14 判断下列句子的语法是否正确。
Decide whether the following statements are grammatically correct (√) or wrong (×).

（1）他很忙。　　　　　（　　　）

（2）这是谁的名片吗?　（　　　）

（3）你去哪儿吗?　　　（　　　）

（4）我去语言学院。　　（　　　）

（5）他汉语学习。　　　（　　　）

15 朗读对话，并回答问题。
Read the dialogue and answer the questions.

林　　娜：我们现在去游泳，好吗?

王小云：对不起，我现在很忙，没有时间。

林　　娜：明天你有时间吗?

王小云：明天我去看京剧，也不行。

问题　Questions

（1）王小云忙吗？

（2）王小云现在有时间去游泳吗？

（3）王小云明天做（zuò, to do）什么？

16 用学过的汉字描述你的一个朋友。（不少于20个字）

Use the characters you have learned to describe one of your friends (more than 20 characters).

17 找句子。

Seek and find.

Try to find as many sentences or questions as possible from the following list of characters. Look horizontally and diagonally. Circle each sentence or question and copy it. For example:

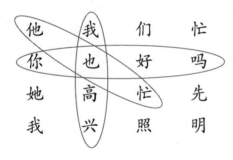

1. 他也忙。

2. 你也好吗？

3. 我也高兴。

（1）
我	认	识	他
介	学	你	听
绍	说	汉	德
一	写	法	语
下	说	英	文

（2）
他	学	美	术
学	法	律	师
经	画	汽	车
济	家	油	子

Nǐmen jiā yǒu jǐ kǒu rén
你们 家 有 几 口 人
How many people are there in your family?

听说练习 Listening and Speaking Exercises

1 发音练习。
Pronunciation drills.

① Read the following phrases, paying attention to the tone sandhis of "不".

不说	不喝	不学	不来	不请	不买
不错	不大	不但	不过	不要	不用
不是	不看	不坐	不介绍	不认识	不太大

② Read the following bisyllabic words, paying attention to the word stress.

1st tone + neutral tone: 妈妈   哥哥   他们

2nd tone + neutral tone: 什么   名字   朋友

3rd tone + neutral tone: 姐姐   我们   你们

4th tone + neutral tone: 爸爸   弟弟   妹妹

③ Read the following numbers, paying attention to the pronunciation of "十".

六	七	八	九	十
十一	十二	十三	十四	十五
三十	五十	七十	六十	九十
二十八	三十五	四十七	六十九	八十三
四十个	五十个	六十张	八十本	九十本
五十一个	二十八个	四十六本	三十七张	八十九张

2 听录音，并回答听到的问题。
Listen and answer the questions you hear.

① _____

② _____

③ _____

④ _____

⑤ _____

⑥ _____

3 听对话，并判断正误。

Listen to the following dialogue and decide whether the statements are true (T) or false (F).

① 这是宋华家的照片。　　　(　　)

② 照片上有五口人。　　　　(　　)

③ 照片上有四口人。　　　　(　　)

④ 小狗是林娜的。　　　　　(　　)

4 听录音，并填空。

Listen and fill in the blanks.

① 我们家有_____人。

② 她是_____。

③ 你们家有_____吗？

④ 你们班_____多少人？

⑤ 你_____学生。

⑥ 我有_____张照片。

5 听录音，写汉字。

Listen and write characters.

6　角色扮演。
Role-play.

Listen to and imitate the dialogue together with your partner.

读写练习　Reading and Writing Exercises

1　按正确的笔顺描汉字，并在后边的空格里写汉字。
Trace over the characters, following the correct stroke order. Then copy the characters in the blank spaces.

几	丿几	几	几						
卜	丨卜	卜	卜						
个	丿人个	个	个						
士	一十士	士	士						
少	丨丨小少	少	少						
欠	丿𠂉欠欠	欠	欠						
云	一二云云	云	云						
禾	一二千禾禾	禾	禾						
未	一二丰未未	未	未						
百	一丆丆百百百	百	百						
两	一丆丙丙丙两两	两	两						
犬	一大大犬	犬	犬						
夕	丿夕夕	夕	夕						

2 在空格里写汉字，注意汉字的部件。

Write the characters in the blank spaces, paying attention to the character components.

jiā	宀＋豕	家								
zhào	日＋刀＋口＋灬	照								
hé	禾＋口	和								
hái	不＋辶	还								
mèi	女＋未	妹								
gòng	廿＋八	共								
gǒu	犭＋勹＋口	狗								
dì	丷＋弔＋丿	弟								
dāng	业＋彐	当								
rán	夕＋犬＋灬	然								
zhēn	十＋且＋八	真								
ài	爫＋冖＋友	爱								
méi	氵＋殳	没								
nán	田＋力	男								
zuò	亻＋古＋攵	做								
zuò	亻＋乍	作								
duō	夕＋夕	多								
wài	夕＋卜	外								

xǐ	士 + 口 + ⸌⸍ + 一 + 口	喜						
huān	又 + 欠	欢						

3 为下列汉字标注拼音，并把它们分解为部件。

Write *pinyin* for the following characters and devide them into character components.

E.g. 谁shéi → 讠 + 隹

（1）张　　　　　　　　（4）谁

（2）教　　　　　　　　（5）请

（3）授　　　　　　　　（6）作

4 选择恰当的汉字填空。

Fill in the blanks with the proper characters.

（1）你们家有_____口人？

　　　A. 心　　　　B. 几　　　　C. 儿

（2）你在哪儿工_____？

　　　A. 做　　　　B. 坐　　　　C. 作

（3）_____是不是你妹妹？

　　　A. 他　　　　B. 她　　　　C. 也

5 根据所给拼音，在第二行中找到能与第一行汉字组成词语的汉字，并连线。

Find a character in the second line which can be combined with a character in the first line to make a word according to the *pinyin* provided. Draw a line to connect the two.

（1）gāoxìng　　（2）jièshào　　（3）xǐhuan　　（4）Hànyǔ　　（5）dāngrán

当　　　介　　　汉　　　喜　　　高

绍　　　兴　　　然　　　语　　　欢

6 根据所给拼音，用括号里的汉字组成句子。

Organize the characters in parentheses into Chinese sentences according to the *pinyin* given.

（1）Wáng Xiǎoyún jiā yǒu sì kǒu rén.

（小云王口人有四家）

_____。

（2）Tāmen yǒu liǎng wèi Zhōngguó lǎoshī.

（两有位他们老师中国）

_____。

（3）Tā gēge zài yīyuàn gōngzuò.

（工作哥哥在他医院）

_____。

（4）Tāmen xuéyuàn yǒu èrshíwǔ ge wàiguó rén.

（有学院他们个二十五外国人）

_____。

（5）Tā hái méiyǒu nán péngyou.

（朋友还男没有她）

_____。

7 为汉字"口"的每一边各加一个部件，组成四个学过的汉字。

Add character components to each side of the character "口" to form four characters which we have learned.

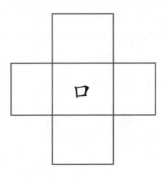

（Key to the riddle in Lesson 7: 一）

8 完成下列对话。

Complete the following dialogues.

（1）A: _____?

B: 我们家有七口人。

（2）A: _____?

B: 我有四个哥哥。

（3）A: _____?

B: 我有很多中国朋友。

（4）A: _____?

B: 我们学校有八十八个中国学生。

（5）A: _____?

B: 他有两张照片。

9 连接 I 和 II 两部分的词语，组成词组。

Match words from part I with those from part II to make phrases.

I	II
一张	个
有	工作
男	姐姐
做什么	朋友
几	照片

10 把下列陈述句变成带"吗"、"几"或"多少"的疑问句。

Change the following statements into questions with "吗", "几" or "多少".

（1）他有很多朋友。→ _____?

（2）我们系有三百人。→ _____?

（3）外语系没有汉语专业。→ _____?

（4）他的弟弟真可爱。→ _____?

（5）我们都喜欢狗。→ _____?

11 用所给词语造句。

Make sentences with the words given.

当然：＿＿＿＿＿＿＿＿＿＿＿＿＿＿＿＿＿＿＿＿

真：＿＿＿＿＿＿＿＿＿＿＿＿＿＿＿＿＿＿＿＿＿

还：＿＿＿＿＿＿＿＿＿＿＿＿＿＿＿＿＿＿＿＿＿

多少：＿＿＿＿＿＿＿＿＿＿＿＿＿＿＿＿＿＿＿＿

12 根据本课课文判断正误。

Decide whether the statements are true (T) or false (F) according to the text of this lesson.

（1）语言学院很大。 　　　　　　（　　）

（2）汉语系的老师有一百多个。 　　（　　）

（3）王小云家有四口人。 　　　　　（　　）

（4）王小云的小猫（māo, cat）叫贝贝。（　　）

（5）林娜的男朋友是老师。 　　　　（　　）

（6）林娜有三个哥哥。 　　　　　　（　　）

13 写一段话描述下列图片。

Write a short paragraph describing the pictures below.

14 判断下列句子的语法是否正确。

Decide whether the statements are grammatically correct (√) or wrong (×).

（1）你们家不有哥哥。 （ 　 ）

（2）你们学校多少有老师？ （ 　 ）

（3）我有一个哥哥，也有一个弟弟。（ 　 ）

（4）我们喜欢狗。 （ 　 ）

（5）她真工作。 （ 　 ）

15 读短文，并回答问题。

Read the passage and answer the questions.

丁力波家有外婆、爸爸、妈妈、哥哥，还有弟弟。他的哥哥是老师。他们都喜欢丁力波。丁力波的爸爸是加拿大人，妈妈是中国人。汉语是他爸爸、妈妈的"介绍人"。

问题　Questions

（1）丁力波家有几口人？

（2）他们都喜欢谁？

（3）"介绍人"是什么意思（yìsi, meaning）？

16 用学过的汉字描述你的家庭。（不少于50个字）

Use the characters you have learned to describe your family (more than 50 characters).

听说练习 *Listening and Speaking Exercises*

1 发音练习。
Pronunciation drills.

Read the following words or phrases, paying attention to the pronunciation of "z, c, s, zh, ch, sh, r".

z	怎么	在北京		
c	参加	餐厅		
s	星期四	二十三	宋华	有意思
zh	祝贺	真漂亮	真高兴	中国人
ch	出生	吃烤鸭	吃寿面	吃蛋糕
sh	上午	寿面	时间	十二号
r	生日	当然	星期日	

2 听问题，并圈出正确的回答。
Listen to each question and circle the correct answer.

15
2~6

①	A. 二十	B. 多大	C. 几岁	D. 有
②	A. 三号	B. 生日	C. 星期	D. 十月
③	A. 学生	B. 下午	C. 上午	D. 没有
④	A. 很好	B. 什么	C. 今天	D. 那儿
⑤	A. 参加	B. 聚会	C. 祝贺	D. 星期

3 听对话，并判断正误。

Listen to the following dialogue and decide whether the statements are true (T) or false (F).

1. 今天是小力的生日。　　　（　　）

2. 今天四月四号。　　　　　（　　）

3. 小力不忙。　　　　　　　（　　）

4. 今天也是小力弟弟的生日。　（　　）

4 听录音，并填空。

Listen and fill in the blanks.

1. 明天_____我有课。

2. 你星期六有_____吗?

3. 你的_____是哪天?

4. 喝红酒，吃_____。

5. 今天是十月_____号。

6. 我_____有时间。

5 听录音，写汉字。

Listen and write characters.

6 角色扮演。

Role-play.

Listen to and imitate the dialogue together with your partner.

7 互动练习：谈论课程表。

Interactions: Talk about this class schedule.

院系：语言学院汉语系

姓名：丁力波

	星期一	星期二	星期三	星期四	星期五
上午	汉语	汉语	中国历史	汉语	汉语
下午	中国美术	中国文学	汉语	中国文化	音乐
晚上		中国哲学（选修）		中国经济（选修）	

Examples:

① A：丁力波星期一上午有没有课？

　　B：他有课。

　　A：他有什么课？

　　B：他有汉语课。

② A：丁力波星期二晚上有时间吗？

　　B：他没有时间，他有中国哲学课。

③ A：丁力波什么时候有中国美术课？

　　B：他星期一下午有中国美术课。

④ A：丁力波的中国历史课在星期几？

　　B：星期三。

8 根据下面的学生卡，和你的语伴一起提问并回答。

Work with your partner, ask and answer questions according to the following student I. D.

经济学院 学生卡
号码：200202

姓　　名：宋华	性　别：男
出生日期：1982年10月27日	出生地：北京市
专　　业：经济法	
住　　址：经济学院学生宿舍3层325号	

 读写练习 Reading and Writing Exercises

1 按正确的笔顺描汉字，并在后边的空格里写汉字。

Trace over the characters, following the correct stroke order. Then copy the characters in the blank spaces.

今	ノ 人 亽 今	今	今					
年	ノ 亠 乍 乍 丘 年	年	年					
果	丨 冂 曰 日 旦 甲 杲 果	果	果					
其	一 十 廿 甘 甘 其 其 其	其	其					
上	丨 卜 上	上	上					
午	ノ 亠 二 午	午	午					
出	乚 屮 屮 出 出	出	出					
尸	㇕ ㇕ 尸	尸	尸					
了	㇇ 了	了	了					

乞	ノ 乛 乞	乞	乞					
虫	丶 口 口 中 虫 虫	虫	虫					
耳	一 丁 丌 丌 丌 耳	耳	耳					
米	丶 丷 半 米 米	米	米					
头	丶 丶 三 头 头	头	头					
瓦	一 丁 瓦 瓦	瓦	瓦					

2 在空格里写汉字，注意汉字的部件。

Write the characters in the blank spaces, paying attention to the character components.

suì	山 + 夕	岁					
zěn	乍 + 心	怎					
yàng	木 + 羊	样					
kè	讠 + 果	课					
xīng	日 + 生	星					
qī	其 + 月	期					
hào	口 + 万	号					
shǔ	尸 + 一 + 虫 + 冂	属					
jù	耳 + 又 + 氺	聚					
huì	人 + 云	会					
zhù	礻 + 兄	祝					

hè	力 ＋ 口 ＋ 贝	贺							
chī	口 ＋ 乞	吃							
mǎi	乛 ＋ 头	买							
píng	⸴ ＋ 开 ＋ 瓦	瓶							
dàn	疋 ＋ 虫	蛋							
gāo	米 ＋ 羔	糕							
hóng	纟 ＋ 工	红							
pú	艹 ＋ 勹 ＋ 甫	葡							
táo	艹 ＋ 勹 ＋ 缶	萄							
jiǔ	氵 ＋ 酉	酒							
cān	厶 ＋ 大 ＋ 彡	参							
sòng	宀 ＋ 木	宋							
huá	亻 ＋ 七 ＋ 十	华							
běi	扌 ＋ 匕	北							
jīng	亠 ＋ 口 ＋ 小	京							

3 把下列汉字分解成部件。

Divide the following characters into character components.

（1）哪　　　　　　（4）咖

（2）娜　　　　　　（5）啊

（3）谢　　　　　　（6）做

4 为每个汉字标注拼音，找到相应的图，并连线。

Give the *pinyin* of the following characters and find the corresponding drawings. Draw a line to connect the two.

（1）头

（2）手

（3）人

（4）耳

（5）目

（6）口

5 根据所给拼音，在第二行中找到能与第一行汉字组成词语的汉字，并连线。

Find a character in the second line which can be combined with a character in the first line to make a word according to the *pinyin* provided. Draw a line to connect the two.

（1）jùhuì　（2）cānjiā　（3）hóngjiǔ　（4）zhùhè　（5）xǐhuan

参　　　聚　　　红　　　祝　　　喜

贺　　　欢　　　加　　　酒　　　会

6 根据所给拼音，用括号里的汉字组成句子。

Organize the characters in parentheses into Chinese sentences according to the *pinyin* given.

（1）Sòng Huá shǔ gǒu, tā jīnnián èrshí suì.

（他狗属宋华二十岁今年）

_____。

（2）Wǒ mǎi liǎng píng hóngpútaojiǔ.

（瓶买两我酒葡萄红）

_____。

（3）Tā xīngqīrì xiàwǔ cānjiā Sòng Huá de shēngri jùhuì.

（星期日下午他聚会生日参加宋华的）

_____。

（4）Lín Nà hěn xǐhuan chī dàngāo.

（很吃喜欢林娜蛋糕）

_____。

7 为"又"的左边和右边各加一个部件，组成两个学过的汉字。

Add character components to each side of the character "又" to form two characters which we have learned.

	又	

（Key to Exercise 7 in Lesson 8: 名、号、加、叫/吗/吃）

8 完成下列对话。

Complete the following dialogues.

（1）A: _____?

　　B: 明天下午我有课。

（2）A: _____?

　　B: 今天是八月一号。

　　A: _____?

　　B: 星期五。

（3）A: _____?

　　　B: 我今年二十岁。

9 连接 I 和 II 两部分的词语，组成词组。

Make phrases by matching words from part Ⅰ with those from part Ⅱ. Draw a line to connect them.

I
吃
祝贺
喝
参加

Ⅱ
聚会
白酒
生日
蛋糕

10 把下列陈述句变成带"吗"的疑问句或是非问句。

Change the following statements into questions with "吗" or V/A-not-V/A questions.

（1）他的生日是一月一号。→ _____?

（2）我买两瓶红酒。→ _____?

（3）明天我有课。→ _____?

（4）生日聚会他们吃寿面。→ _____?

（5）我生日很快乐。→ _____?

11 用所给词语造句。

Make sentences with the words given.

多大: _____

快乐: _____

漂亮: _____

买: _____

祝贺: _____

12　根据本课课文判断正误。

Decide whether the statements are true (T) or false (F) according to the text of this lesson.

（1）宋华是上海人。　　　　　　　　（　　）

（2）宋华今年二十二岁。　　　　　　（　　）

（3）星期四下午我们有个聚会。　　　（　　）

（4）宋华的生日是十月七号。　　　　（　　）

（5）中国人过生日吃寿面。　　　　　（　　）

13　写一段话描述下列图片。

Write a short paragraph describing the pictures below.

14　判断下列句子的语法是否正确。

Decide whether the statements are grammatically correct (√) or wrong (✕).

（1）他今年多岁?　　　　（　　）

（2）他今年多大?　　　　（　　）

（3）我们买大一个蛋糕。　（　　）

（4）明天二十三号十月。　（　　）

（5）我喜欢很烤鸭。　　　（　　）

15 读对话，并回答问题。

Read the passage and answer the questions.

今天是十月一号，是小王的生日。他的朋友都来参加生日聚会。朋友们买很多礼物（lǐwù, gift）来参加聚会：有红葡萄酒，有烤鸭，还有大蛋糕。大家（dàjiā, all the people）都很高兴。

问题 Questions

（1）今天是几月几号？

（2）朋友们参加什么活动（huódòng, activity）？

（3）他们买什么去参加活动？

（4）大家高兴不高兴？

16 用学过的汉字描述你自己。（不少于50个字）

Use the characters you have learned to describe yourself (more than 50 characters).

17 阅读下列材料，并做练习。

Read the following materials and do the exercises.

（1）Read the following clipping from the Chinese newspaper 人民日报 (Rénmín Rìbào, *People's Daily*) and fill in the following blanks.

This newspaper was issued（in Beijing）on:

Date / month / year: _____

Day of the week: _____

（2）Circle or highlight the characters in this newspaper clipping that you have learned so far.

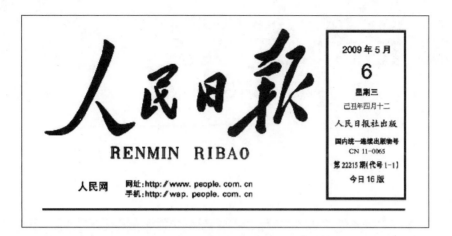

（3）Read the following clipping from the Chinese newspaper 北京青年报（Běijīng Qīngnián Bào，*Beijing Youth Daily*）and fill in the following blanks.

This newspaper was issued（in Beijing）on:

Date / month / year: _____

Day of the week: _____

（4）Circle or highlight the characters in this newspaper clipping that you have learned so far.

Wǒ zài zhèr mǎi guāngpán
我 在 这儿买 光盘
I am here to buy a CD.

听说练习 Listening and Speaking Exercises

1 发音练习。
Pronunciation drills.

Read the following words or phrases, paying attention to the pronunciation of "b, p, d, t, g, k".

b	书报	北京	本子	丁力波	抱歉
p	外婆	葡萄	苹果	漂亮	朋友
d	多少	蛋糕	马大为	大商场	对不起
t	听课	餐厅	太贵	星期天	昨天
g	光盘	工作	高兴	一共	中国音乐
k	咖啡	看书	三块	恐怕	可是

16
2~6
2 听录音，并回答听到的问题。
Listen and answer the questions you hear.

1 _____

2 _____

3 _____

4 _____

5 _____

3 听对话，并判断正误。

Listen to the following dialogue and decide whether the statements are true (T) or false (F).

① 皮鞋（píxié, leather shoes）很贵。 （ ）

② 皮鞋和包（bāo, bag）一共三百块钱。 （ ）

③ 顾客（gùkè, customer）没有买包。 （ ）

4 听录音，并填空。

Listen and fill in the blanks.

① 你还要_____？

② 再_____你一个橘子（júzi, orange）。

③ 我给你_____。

④ 一共_____？

⑤ 这家商店很_____。

5 听录音，写汉字。

Listen and write characters.

6 角色扮演。

Role-play.

Listen to and imitate the dialogue together with your partner. Try to get the meaning of the dialogue with the help of your friends, teachers, or dictionaries.

 读写练习　Reading and Writing Exercises

1 按正确的笔顺描汉字，并在后边的空格里写汉字。

Trace over the characters, following the correct stroke order. Then copy the characters in the blank spaces.

舟	´ ノ 丿 月 舟 舟	舟	舟				
皿	丨 冂 皿 皿 皿	皿	皿				
乐	´ 亠 乐 乐 乐	乐	乐				
书	¬ 乛 书 书	书	书				
本	一 十 才 木 本	本	本				
足	丨 口 口 甲 무 足 足	足	足				
平	´ 一 一 平 平	平	平				
走	一 十 土 キ キ 走 走	走	走				
己	¬ コ 己	己	己				
金	ノ 人 人 今 全 全 金 金	金	金				
斤	´ 厂 斤 斤	斤	斤				
毛	´ 二 三 毛	毛	毛				
戈	一 弋 戈 戈	戈	戈				
穴	´ ´ 宀 穴 穴	穴	穴				
勿	´ 勺 勺 勿	勿	勿				

2 在空格里写汉字，注意汉字的部件。

Write the characters in the blank spaces, paying attention to the character components.

guāng	业 + 儿	光							
pán	舟 + 皿	盘							
yīn	立 + 日	音							
duì	又 + 寸	对							
qǐ	走 + 己	起							
shāng	一 + 丷 + 冂 + 八 + 口	商							
chǎng	土 + 昜	场							
cháng	宀 + 口 + 巾	常							
bào	扌 + 卩 + 又	报							
gěi	纟 + 人 + 一 + 口	给							
gēn	𧾷 + 艮	跟							
liáng	氵 + 刅 + 木	梁							
yào	西 + 女	要							
xiān	生 + 儿	先							
xiāng	禾 + 日	香							
jiāo	艹 + 隹 + 灬	蕉							
píng	艹 + 平	苹							
róng	宀 + 八 + 口	容							

yì	日 + 勿	易							
qián	钅 + 一 + 戈	钱							
kuài	土 + 夬	块							
fēn	八 + 刀	分							
fù	亻 + 甫 + 寸	傅							
sòng	丷 + 天 + 辶	送							
zhǎo	扌 + 戈	找							

3 把下列汉字分解成部件。

Divide the following characters into character components.

（1）是　　　　　　　　（6）思

（2）星　　　　　　　　（7）意

（3）兴　　　　　　　　（8）贵

（4）爸　　　　　　　　（9）高

（5）家　　　　　　　　（10）京

4 为每个汉字标注拼音，找到相应的图片，并连线。

Give *pinyin* of the following characters and find the corresponding drawings. Draw a line to connect the two.

（1）山

（2）日

（3）月

（4）马

（5）水

（6）木

（7）竹

（8）犬

（9）羊

（10）牛

5 根据所给拼音，在第二行中找到能与第一行汉字组成词语的汉字，并连线。

Find a character in the second line which can be combined with a character in the first line to make a word according to the *pinyin* provided. Draw a line to connect the two.

（1）pútao （2）xiāngjiāo （3）píngguǒ （4）xiānsheng （5）xiǎojie

香　苹　葡　小　先

生　蕉　果　萄　姐

6 根据所给拼音，用括号里的汉字造句。

Organize the characters in parentheses into Chinese sentences according to the *pinyin* given.

（1）Pútao duōshao qián yì jīn?

　　（多少葡萄一斤钱）

　　_____?

（2）Píngguǒ wǔ kuài qián liǎng jīn.

　　（五块苹果钱斤两）

　　_____。

（3）Wǒ gěi nǐ wǔshí kuài.

　　（给五十你块我）

　　_____。

（4）Wǒ zhǎo nǐ shísì kuài wǔ máo.

　　（找你我十四块五毛）

　　_____。

7 完成下列短文。

Complete the following passage.

　　　　我们家有_____口人：爸爸、妈妈、_____和我。我爸爸

是_____，妈妈是_____。他们都很忙。_____月_____日

星期_____是我的生日。我属_____，今年_____岁。

8 在空格里填上一个部件，使它和其他部件组成三个学过的汉字。

Fill in the blank with a character component to form three characters which we have learned.

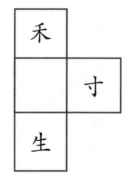

（Key to Exercise 7 in Lesson 9: 汉、对）

9 完成下列对话。
Complete the following dialogues.

（1）A: _____?

　　　B: 这叫香蕉苹果。

（2）A: _____?

　　　B: 八十六块。

（3）A: _____?

　　　B: 这儿没有报纸。

（4）A: _____?

　　　B: 我喜欢音乐光盘。

10 连接 I 和 II 两部分的词语，组成词组。
Make phrases by matching words from part Ⅰ with those from part Ⅱ. Draw a line to connect them.

11 把下列陈述句变为带疑问代词的疑问句。
Change the following statements into questions with interrogative pronouns.

（1）"Study"，汉语是"学习"。→ _____?

（2）她在商场工作。→ _____?

（3）一斤苹果两块五毛钱。→ _____?

（4）他送我一张光盘。→ _____?

（5）他们是医生。→ _____?

12 用所给词语造句。
Make sentences with the words given.

有名：_____

跟：_____

常常：_____

在：_____

送：_____

13 根据本课课文判断正误。
Decide whether the statements are true (T) or false (F) according to the text of this lesson.

（1）马大为在商场买苹果。　　　（　　）

（2）马大为不喜欢中国音乐。　　　（　　）

（3）马大为要买本子。　　　（　　）

（4）丁力波问苹果多少钱一斤。　　　（　　）

（5）一斤香蕉苹果两块七毛五分。　　（　　）

14 写一段话描述下列图片。
Write a short paragraph describing the pictures below.

15 判断下列句子的语法是否正确。

Decide whether the statements are grammatically correct (√) or wrong (✕).

（1）你还要什么？ 　　　　　　（　　）

（2）我有三毛两块钱。 　　　　　（　　）

（3）你跟我学。 　　　　　　　　（　　）

（4）你给十块钱我。 　　　　　　（　　）

16 朗读短文，并回答问题。

Read the passage and answer the questions.

在中国买东西

　　林娜常常去中国商场买东西，她喜欢买光盘和葡萄酒。她常常问售货员："这张光盘多少钱？""那瓶葡萄酒多少钱？""这个汉语怎么说？"她的汉语不太好，常常要问很多遍（biàn，time）。中国的售货员很有耐心（nàixīn，patient），他们也喜欢和她说汉语。

问题　Questions

（1）林娜常常去哪儿？

（2）林娜为什么要问很多遍？

（3）售货员喜欢和她说汉语吗？

17 用学过的汉字描述一次购物的经历。（不少于50个字）

Use the characters you have learned to describe a shopping experience (more than 50 characters).

18 读下列材料，并做练习。
Read the following materials and do the exercises.

（1）Read the following clipping from a Chinese

periodical and find out:

a. The name of this Chinese periodical:

_____

b. The price of this periodical:

_____

c. The date this periodical was issued:

_____

（2）Read the following receipt for "China Card" telephone fee and find out:

a. The serial number of the receipt: _____

b. The amount of the call fee: _____

c. The date of the receipt: _____

北京长途电话局   (2)
Beijing Long Distance Telephone Bureau

流水号: 0610978
Serial Number

中国电话卡话费收据
Receipt of China Card Telephone Fee

姓 名_____   话费金额(小写)_____
Name   Call Fee (in small letter)

话费金额(大写)___佰___拾___万___仟___佰___拾___圆___分
Call Fee (in capital letter)

收款员_____   日期: 2009 年___ 月___ 日
Money Collector   Date: Day   Month   Year

（3）Read the following advertisement and find out the prices of the following items.

Item 0862: _____   Item 0821: _____

Item 0855: _____   Item 0824: _____

Item 0861: _____   Item 0827: _____

0861 ￥2.6	0862 ￥2.2	0824 ￥3.2	0827 ￥3.2
蒙牛纯牛奶 250ml/盒	伊利高钙奶 250ml/袋	白玉黑豆豆浆 330ml/瓶	蒙牛凝固型原味酸牛奶 180g/杯
一级 积分:2	一级 积分:2	积分:3	一级 积分:2

0828 ￥2.0	0822 ￥2.4	0821 ￥2.5	0855 ￥3.2
蒙牛冠益乳原味酸牛奶 100g/杯	三元金丝红枣酸牛奶 180g/杯	三元纯牛奶 250ml/盒	光明草莓味特浓酸牛奶 200g/盒
一级 积分:2	一级 积分:2	一级 积分:2	一级 积分:3

（4）Read the following advertisement for a book club and find out the prices of the following items.

Item 04499: _____   Item 03087: _____

Item 01495: _____   Item 04481: _____

Can you figure out any other information?

_____

_____

如今学习英语在全国蔚然成风。本书是一本专为出国留学生编写的口语教材，汇集了留学生非常熟悉的课内外生活的方方面面。融实用性、知识性于一体，以便给大家提供一个练习口语的机会。本书细分了九个主题，包括留学准备、入学、校园活动等。

在内容编排上，每部分分为四个章节"热身句型"、"精彩表达"、"身临其境"、"词海拾贝"，让你掌握地道的英语。

定价：￥33.50
25.20元
03087   16开   181页

自1947年出版，已翻译成50多种文字，全球畅销几千万册。在欧洲被誉为第二次世界大战以来影响世界的100部书之一。

一个16岁的少女，最大的愿望是做一名记者和作家，却因为希特勒发动的一场邪恶的战争，于花季之龄死于纳粹集中营。日记是安妮遇难前两年藏身密室时的生活和情感的记载，反映了在种族歧视和战争迫害的社会大环境中，藏匿且充满恐怖。

定价：￥28.80
24.00元
02444   16开   312页

◎畅销全球80国的世界级励志书！
◎世界500强企业团购率第1名！
◎美国亚马逊、台湾金石堂、诚品书店心灵励志新书销量第1名！
◎《纽约时报》、《时代周刊》、《芝加哥太阳报》、NBC电视台……全球超过100家重量级媒体专题报导！
◆一本书，一只手环，改变爱抱怨的你，成就不抱怨的世界。
◆不抱怨与团队：任何人和团队要想成功，就永远不要抱怨，因为抱怨不如改变，要有接纳批评的包容心，以及解决问题的行动力！

大32开　223页

定价：￥24.80
16.00元
01495

龙应台的文字，"横眉冷对千夫指"时，寒气逼人，如刀光剑影。"俯首甘为孺子牛"时，却温柔婉转仿佛微风吹过麦田。从纯真喜悦的《孩子你慢慢来》到坦率得近乎"痛楚"的《亲爱的安德烈》，龙应台的写作境界逐渐转往人生的深沉。

《目送》的七十四篇散文，写父亲的逝、母亲的老、儿子的离、朋友的牵挂、兄弟的携手共行，写失败和脆弱、失落和放手，写缠绵不舍和绝然的虚无。

这是一本生死笔记，深邃、忧伤、美丽。

16开　281页

定价：￥39.00
29.10元
04507

苏菲的世界

◎一本风靡世界的哲学启蒙书
◎已翻译成54种语言出版
◎全球销售超过三亿册
◎获挪威、德国、西班牙等国图书大奖

14岁的少女苏菲不断接到一些极不寻常的来信，世界像谜团一般在她眼前展开。在一位神秘导师的指引下，苏菲开始思索，她运用少女天生的悟性与后天知识，企图解开这些谜团……

《苏菲的世界》，是智慧的世界，梦的世界。它将会唤醒每个人内心深处对生命的赞叹与对人生终极意义的关怀与好奇。

32开　528页

定价：￥26.00
17.40元
04499

关于爱、友情以及永不磨灭的信仰！

本书足以改变读者一生的心灵，全球读者口耳相传，渴望与最爱的人分享！

《时代》、《纽约时报》、《出版人周刊》……全球顶级媒体鼎力推荐！畅销11国，感动世界的文学经典，你一定被感动！

我们每个人都在寻觅心中尚未崩塌的地方，过上自己想要的生活，那就是没有悲伤的城市。

本书来到你身边，和你分享所有的感动和爱。

大32开　254页

定价：￥25.00
14.40元
04481

A Summary of Questions with an Interrogative Pronoun

We have studied many questions with an interrogative pronoun. The word order of this kind of sentence is the same as that of a declarative sentence. In other words, a declarative sentence can be easily changed into this kind of question by replacing the relevant sentence element with its corresponding interrogative pronoun.

Interrogative pronoun	Statement	Question
谁 who	那是马小姐。 他是我们老师。 这是张教授的名片。	那是谁? 谁是我们老师? 这是谁的名片?
什么 what	这是苹果。 他学习美术专业。	这是什么? 他学习什么专业?
哪 which	我是中国人。	您是哪国人?
哪儿 where	他是北京人。 她在这儿。 我在美术学院学习。	他是哪儿人? 她在哪儿? 您在哪儿学习?
怎么样 How is it?	这张光盘很好。	这张光盘怎么样?
怎么 how	这叫苹果。	这个汉语怎么说?
几 how many; how much	我们家有五口人。 今天十月二十四号。 明天星期六。	你们家有几口人? 今天几号? 明天星期几?
多少 how many; how much	我们系有二十八位老师。 一斤苹果三块五毛钱。	你们系有多少老师? 一斤苹果多少钱?

Wǒ huì shuō yìdiǎnr Hànyǔ
我 会 说 一点儿 汉语
I can speak a little Chinese.

听说练习 Listening and Speaking Exercises

1 发音练习。
Pronunciation drills.

Read the following words or phrases aloud, paying special attention to the pronunciation of "e, u, ie, üe, uo, ou".

e	上课	哥哥	这个
u	五点	不贵	岁数
ie	小姐	也喜欢	写汉字
üe	学院	学习	学英语
uo	多少	工作	我们
ou	都好	头疼	走路

2 听录音，并回答听到的问题。
Listen and answer the questions you hear.

17
2~6

1 _____

2 _____

3 _____

4 _____

5 _____

3 听对话，并判断正误。

Listen to the following dialogue and decide whether the statements are true (T) or false (F).

① 女士（nǚshì, the lady）八点半上课。　　　（　　）

② 现在七点。　　　　　　　　　　　　　　（　　）

③ 司机可以开（kāi，to drive）快（kuài, fast）点儿。（　　）

4 听录音，并填空。

Listen and fill in the blanks.

① 我会说＿＿＿＿＿＿＿＿＿＿＿汉语。

② 你们＿＿＿＿＿＿＿＿＿＿＿上课。

③ 现在＿＿＿＿＿＿＿＿＿＿＿。

④ 我的＿＿＿＿＿＿＿＿＿＿＿不好。

⑤ 我＿＿＿＿＿＿＿＿＿＿＿来。

5 听录音，写汉字。

Listen and write characters.

6 角色扮演。

Role-play.

Listen to and imitate the dialogue together with your partner. Try to get the meaning of the dialogue with the help of your friends, teachers or dictionaries.

7 互动练习：和你的语伴一起谈论时间表。

Interactions: Talk about your timetable together with your partner.

星期五　　　7：00　起床

　　　　　　7：30　吃早饭

　　　　　　8：00—12：00　上课

　　　　　　12：30　吃午饭

　　　　　　14：00—16：30　上课

　　　　　　17：00　打球

　　　　　　18：00　吃晚饭

　　　　　　19：00—21：00　看书

　　　　　　21：30—22：30　跳舞

　　　　　　23：00　睡觉

星期六　　　8：00　起床

　　　　　　8：30　吃早饭

　　　　　　9：30　去商场买东西

　　　　　　11：00　游泳

　　　　　　12：30　吃午饭

　　　　　　14：00　参加朋友的聚会

　　　　　　17：30　回宿舍

　　　　　　18：00　吃晚饭

　　　　　　19：00—21：00　写汉字

　　　　　　21：30—22：30　听音乐

　　　　　　23：00　睡觉

 读写练习 *Reading and Writing Exercises*

1 按正确的笔顺描汉字，并在后边的空格里写汉字。
Trace over the characters, following the correct stroke order. Then copy the characters in the blank spaces.

占	`丨卜 ㅏ 占 占`	占	占				
里	`丨冂曰日甲甲里`	里	里				
央	`丨冂凸央央`	央	央				
至	`一厶互互至至`	至	至				
东	`一厂厇东东`	东	东				
西	`一冂冂冋両西`	西	西				
免	`ノ夕夕夕免免免`	免	免				
半	`丶丷丷半半`	半	半				
与	`一与与`	与	与				
页	`一丆丆页页页`	页	页				
以	`丶丷以以`	以	以				

2 在空格里写汉字，注意汉字的部件。
Write the characters in the blank spaces, paying attention to the character components.

| sī | `ㄱ + 一 + 口` | 司 | | | | | | |

jī	木 + 几	机							
diǎn	占 + 灬	点							
zhōng	钅 + 中	钟							
chà	羊 + 工	差							
kè	亥 + 刂	刻							
huí	囗 + 口	回							
yīng	艹 + 央	英							
sūn	孑 + 小	孙							
shù	米 + 女 + 攵	数							
dào	至 + 刂	到							
bài	手 + 一 + 丰	拜							
néng	厶 + 月 + 匕 + 匕	能							
zuó	日 + 乍	昨							
wán	王 + 元	玩							
xiě	宀 + 与	写							
wǎn	日 + 免	晚							
shuì	目 + 千 + 艹 + 二	睡							
jiào	灬 + 见	觉							
chuáng	广 + 木	床							

yīng	广 + 业	应							
gāi	讠 + 亥	该							
tí	是 + 页	题							
chén	阝 + 东	陈							

3 把下列汉字分解成部件。

Divide the following characters into character components.

（1）国　　　　　　　　（5）属

（2）回　　　　　　　　（6）医

（3）问　　　　　　　　（7）可

（4）用　　　　　　　　（8）司

4 根据拼音写汉字。

Write characters according to the *pinyin*.

（1）天：zuótiān_____　　jīntiān_____　　míngtiān_____

（2）年：qùnián_____　　jīnnián_____　　míngnián_____

（3）午：shàngwǔ_____　　zhōngwǔ_____　　xiàwǔ_____

（4）学：xiǎoxué_____　　zhōngxué_____　　dàxué_____

5 为每个汉字标注拼音，找到相应的图片，并连线。

Give the *pinyin* of the following characters and find the corresponding drawings.
Draw a line to connect the two.

（1）下

（2）上

（3）门

（4）弓

（5）犬

（6）虫

（7）刀

（8）云

（9）井

（10）心

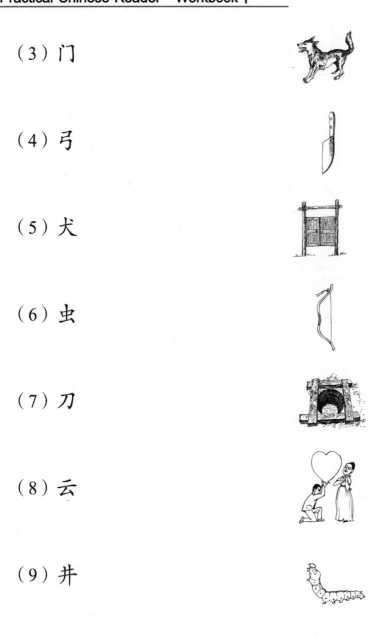

6 根据所给拼音，用括号里的汉字组成句子。
Organize the characters in parentheses into Chinese sentences according to the *pinyin* given.

（1）Qǐngwèn, shàngwǔ jǐ diǎn shàng Hànyǔ kè?

（上课请问几点上午汉语）

_____?

（2）Wǒmen shí diǎn shàng Hànyǔ kè.

（十点上汉语我们课）

_____。

（3）Tā xiàwǔ liǎng diǎn bàn yǒu yí ge jùhuì.

（他下午有两点半聚会一个）

_____。

（4）Nǐ míngtiān wǎnshang néng huí jiā ma?

（明天晚上能你家回吗）

_____？

7 用汉字列出你的课程表。
Write a timetable of your classes in characters.

8 猜字谜。
Character riddle.

一字有两口，大口吃小口。

（The key is a character.）

（Key to Exercise 8 in Lesson 10: 日）

9 完成下列对话。

Complete the following dialogues.

（1）A: _____?

　　B: 我会说汉语。

（2）A: _____?

　　B: 她能来上课。

（3）A: _____?

　　B: 我七点能到。

（4）A: _____?

　　B: 我差一刻七点起床。

（5）A: _____?

　　B: 当然可以。

（6）A: _____?

　　B: 我们八点上课。

10 连接 I 和 II 两部分的词语，组成词组。

Make phrases by matching words from part I with those from part II. Draw a line to connect them.

11 把下列陈述句变成带"吗"的疑问句。

Change the following statements into questions with "吗".

（1）她会说汉语。→ _____?

（2）他能来。→ _____?

（3）他会游泳。→ _____？

（4）你可以去看京剧。→ _____？

（5）他应该现在起床。→ _____？

12 用所给词语造句。
Make sentences with the words given.

能：_____

会：_____

几点：_____

为什么：_____

写：_____

可以：_____

13 根据本课课文判断正误。
Decide whether the statements are true (T) or false (F) according to the text of this lesson.

（1）马大为能来上课。 　　　　　（　　）

（2）马大为十点回学校。 　　　　　（　　）

（3）司机不会说英语。 　　　　　（　　）

（4）马大为不应该上课。 　　　　　（　　）

（5）马大为下午去商场买东西。 　　（　　）

14 写一段话描述下列图片。
Write a short paragraph describing the picture below.

15 判断下列句子的语法是否正确。
Decide whether the statements are grammatically correct (√) or wrong (×).

（1）我说英语会。　　　　　　（　　　）

（2）今天能我不来上课。　　　（　　　）

（3）今天我不能来上课。　　　（　　　）

（4）十一半点。　　　　　　　（　　　）

（5）十一点半。　　　　　　　（　　　）

16 读短文，并回答问题。
Read the passage and answer the questions.

我能说汉语

丁力波能说英语，也能说汉语。他的妈妈是中国人。

星期六，丁力波去买书，他对售货员说："我要一本法语书。"售货员给他一本书，他很高兴。力波回到家，他妈妈问他："你买了什么书？"力波说："法语书。"妈妈说："你看，这是法语书吗？你能说汉语，可是不认识汉字，这是法律（fǎlǜ, law）书，不是法语书。""啊？！"

问题　Questions

（1）丁力波要买法律书还是法语书？

（2）售货员给他一本什么书？

17 用学过的汉字描述一次有趣的经历。（不少于50个字）
Use the characters you have learned to describe an interesting experience you have learned (more than 50 characters).

18 阅读下列材料，并做练习。
Read the following materials and do the exercises.

（1）Read the following Chart of Standard World Time and find out what time it is now in the following cities.

北京（Beijing）：＿＿＿＿＿＿　　温哥华（Vancouver）：＿＿＿＿＿＿

东京（Tokyo）：＿＿＿＿＿＿　　莫斯科（Moscow）：＿＿＿＿＿＿

伦敦（London）：＿＿＿＿＿＿　　华盛顿（Washington）：＿＿＿＿＿＿

世界标准时间　Standard World Time

City	城　市	Greenwich Mean Time	City	城　市	Greenwich Mean Time	City	城　市	Greenwich Mean Time
Accra(Ghana)	阿克拉(加纳)	12:00	Delhi(India)	德里(印度)	17:30	Munich(Germany)	慕尼黑(德国)	15:00
Addis Ababa(Ethiopia)	亚的斯亚贝巴(埃塞俄比亚)	15:00	Detroit(USA)	底特律(美国)	07:00	Nairobi(Kenya)	内罗毕(肯尼亚)	15:00
Adelaide(Australia)	阿德莱德(澳大利亚)	21:30	Dubai(UAE)	迪拜(阿联酋)	16:00	Naples(Italy)	那不勒斯(意大利)	13:00
Aden(Yemen)	亚丁(也门)	15:00	Dublin(Ireland)	都柏林(爱尔兰)	12:00	New York(USA)	纽约(美国)	07:00
Alexandria(Egypt)	亚历山大(埃及)	14:00	Frankfurt(Germany)	法兰克福(德国)	13:00	Osaka(Japan)	大阪(日本)	21:00
Algiers(Algeria)	阿尔及尔(阿尔及利亚)	13:00	Geneva(Switzerland)	日内瓦(瑞士)	13:00	Ottawa(Canada)	渥太华(加拿大)	07:00
Amsterdam(Netherlands)	阿姆斯特丹(荷兰)	13:00	Guadalajara(Mexico)	瓜达拉哈拉(墨西哥)	05:00	Panama City(Panama)	巴拿马城(巴拿马)	06:00
Amkara(Turkey)	安卡拉(土耳其)	14:00	Hamburg(Germany)	汉堡(德国)	13:00	Pairs(France)	巴黎(法国)	13:00
Athens(Greece)	雅典(希腊)	14:00	Hanoi(Vietnam)	河内(越南)	19:00	Philadelphia(USA)	费城(美国)	07:00
Auckland(New Zealand)	奥克兰(新西兰)	24:00	Havanna(Cuba)	哈瓦那(古巴)	07:00	Pittsburgh(USA)	匹兹堡(美国)	07:00
Baghdad(Iraq)	巴格达(伊拉克)	15:00	Helsinki(Finland)	赫尔辛基(芬兰)	14:00	Prague(Czechoslavakia)	布拉格(捷克和斯洛伐克)	13:00
Baltimore(USA)	巴尔的摩(美国)	07:00	Ho Chi Minh City(Vietnam)	胡志明市(越南)	19:00	Pusan(S.Korea)	釜山(韩国)	21:00
Bandar Seri Begawan(Brunei)	斯里巴加湾港(文莱)	20:00	Honolulu(USA)	檀香山(美国)	02:00	Pyongyang(Korea)	平壤(朝鲜)	21:00
Bandung(Indonesia)	万隆(印度尼西亚)	19:00	Islamabad(Pakistan)	伊斯兰堡(巴基斯坦)	17:00	Quebec(Canada)	魁北克(加拿大)	07:00
Bangkok(Thailand)	曼谷(泰国)	19:00	Istanbul(Turkey)	伊斯坦布尔(土耳其)	14:00	Rangoon(Burma)	仰光(缅甸)	18:30
Barcelona(Spain)	巴塞罗那(西班牙)	13:00	Jakarta(Indonesia)	雅加达(印度尼西亚)	19:00	Rio de Janeiro(Brazil)	里约热内卢(巴西)	09:00
Beijing(China)	北京(中国)	20:00	Jeddah(Saudi,Arabia)	吉达(沙特阿拉伯)	15:00	Rome(Italy)	罗马(意大利)	13:00
Beirut(Lebanon)	贝鲁特(黎巴嫩)	14:00	Kabul(Afghanistan)	喀布尔(阿富汗)	16:30	Rotterdam(Netherlands)	鹿特丹(荷兰)	13:00
Belgrade(Yugoslavia)	贝尔格莱德(南斯拉夫)	13:00	Karachi(Pakistan)	卡拉奇(巴基斯坦)	17:00	San Francisco(USA)	旧金山(美国)	04:00
Berlin(Germany)	柏林(德国)	13:00	Katmandu(Nepal)	加德满都(尼泊尔)	17:30	Santiago(Chile)	圣地亚哥(智利)	08:00
Berne(Switzerland)	伯尔尼(瑞士)	13:00	Kinshasa(Zaire)	金沙萨(扎伊尔)	13:00	Sao Paulo(Brazil)	圣保罗(巴西)	09:00
Bombay(India)	孟买(印度)	17:00	Kowloon(Hong Kong)	九龙(中国香港)	20:00	Seoul(S.Korea)	汉城(韩国)	21:00
Bonn(Germany)	波恩(德国)	13:00	Kuala Lumpur(Malaysia)	吉隆坡(马来西亚)	20:00	Singapore(Singapore)	新加坡(新加坡)	20:00
Boston(USA)	波士顿(美国)	07:00	Kuwait(Kuwait)	科威特(科威特)	15:00	Sofia(Bulgaria)	索菲亚(保加利亚)	14:00
Brazzaville(Congo)	布拉柴维尔(刚果)	13:00	Kyoto(Japan)	京都(日本)	21:00	Stockholm(Sweden)	斯德哥尔摩(瑞典)	13:00
Brussels(Belgium)	布鲁塞尔(比利时)	13:00	Lagos(Nigeria)	拉各斯(尼日利亚)	13:00	Suez(Egypt)	苏伊士(埃及)	14:00
Bucharest(Romania)	布加勒斯特(罗马尼亚)	14:00	Leningrad(CIS)	列宁格勒(独联体)	15:00	Sydney(Australia)	悉尼(澳大利亚)	22:00
Budapest(Hungary)	布达佩斯(匈牙利)	13:00	Lima(Peru)	利马(秘鲁)	07:00	Tehran(Iran)	德黑兰(伊朗)	15:30
Buenos Aires(Argentina)	布宜诺斯艾利斯(阿根廷)	09:00	Lisbon(Portugal)	里斯本(葡萄牙)	12:00	Tokyo(Japan)	东京(日本)	21:00
Cairo(Egypt)	开罗(埃及)	14:00	London(UK)	伦敦(英国)	12:00	Toronto(Canada)	多伦多(加拿大)	07:00
Calcutta(India)	加尔各答(印度)	17:30	Los Angeles(USA)	洛杉矶(美国)	04:00	Tunis(Tunisia)	突尼斯(突尼斯)	13:00
Canberra(Australia)	堪培拉(澳大利亚)	22:00	Madrid(Spain)	马德里(西班牙)	13:00	Vancouver(Canada)	温哥华(加拿大)	04:00
Caracas(Venezuela)	加拉加斯(委内瑞拉)	08:00	Malta(Malta)	马耳他(马耳他)	13:00	Vienna(Austria)	维也纳(奥地利)	13:00
Chicago(USA)	芝加哥(美国)	06:00	Manila(Philippines)	马尼拉(菲律宾)	20:00	Warsaw(Poland)	华沙(波兰)	13:00
Cologne(Germany)	科隆(德国)	13:00	Melbourne(Australia)	墨尔本(澳大利亚)	22:00	Washington(USA)	华盛顿(美国)	07:00
Colombo(Sri Lanka)	科伦坡(斯里兰卡)	17:30	Mexico City(Mexico)	墨西哥城(墨西哥)	06:00	Wellington(New Zealand)	惠灵顿(新西兰)	24:00
Copenhagen(Denmark)	哥本哈根(丹麦)	13:00	Miami(USA)	迈阿密(美国)	07:00	Winnipeg(Canada)	温尼伯(加拿大)	06:00
Dacca(Bangladesh)	达卡(孟加拉)	18:00	Milan(Italy)	米兰(意大利)	13:00	Zurich(Switzerland)	苏黎士(瑞士)	13:00
Damascus(Syria)	大马士革(叙利亚)	14:00	Montreal(Canada)	蒙特利尔(加拿大)	07:00			
Darwin(Australia)	达尔文(澳大利亚)	21:30	Moscow(CIS)	莫斯科(俄罗斯)	15:00			

It is noon of Greenwich Mean Time in the table. 表中时间为格林尼治正午时间。

（2）Read the following train schedule from Beijing Train Station and find out the departure time or arrival time of the following trains.

Departure Time:

K45: _____　　　　　1461: _____

T31: _____　　　　　D11: _____

K107: _____　　　　　Z15: _____

Arrival Time:

T59: _____　　　　　Z61: _____

T65: _____　　　　　D309: _____

K681: _____　　　　　2189: _____

Note: "开点", departure time; "到点", arrival time.

北京站部分始发列车时刻表

车次	开点	到站	到点	车次	开点	到站	到点
N211	06:30	承德	当日10:48	K107	17:48	徐州	次日05:54
D25	07:15	哈尔滨	当日15:19	T228	18:16	大连	次日05:38
D21	07:20	长春	当日13:40	K263	18:48	包头	次日07:19
Y509	07:50	秦皇岛	当日11:11	T271	19:10	吉林	次日06:16
4405	09:01	天津	当日10:53	Z7	19:44	上海	次日07:12
D5	09:20	沈阳北	当日13:31	Z85	19:50	苏州	次日06:40
4419	10:03	唐山	当日14:21	T109	20:02	上海	次日09:19
1301	10:50	满洲里	当日17:54	K601	20:30	太原	次日07:28
K45	11:45	福州	当日21:18	T59	21:00	长春	次日06:10
K43B	12:03	兰州	次日15:15	Z15	21:20	哈尔滨	次日07:04
D11	13:55	沈阳北	当日18:06	D309	21:34	杭州	次日09:01
1461	14:42	上海	次日12:49	D301	21:39	上海	次日07:38
4415	15:06	张家口	当日20:08	Z73	21:50	合肥	次日07:12
4495	15:22	秦皇岛	当日19:11	K681	21:57	大连	次日08:08
2189	15:30	乌兰浩特	次日10:21	Z49	22:02	南京	次日07:14
T31	15:39	杭州	次日06:26	T63	22:08	合肥	次日09:08
K161	16:00	南京西	次日07:30	T65	22:14	南京西	次日09:13
K285	16:30	烟台	次日06:30	K53	22:15	沈阳北	次日07:25
4401	16:36	天津	当日18:36	Z61	22:40	长春	次日06:30
D23	17:20	长春	当日23:23	T25	22:50	青岛	次日07:22

（3）Read the following Beijing Taxi Receipt and find out:

a. When the passenger got into the taxi:

_____

b. When the passenger got out of the taxi:

_____

c. The total amount of fee: _____

d. The date of the receipt: _____

e. The telephone number of the taxi company:

_____

f. Can you figure out any other information?

_____

_____

北京出租车专用发票
BEIJING TAXI SPECIAL INVOICE
发票联
INVOICE

211000911013
47546099

单位　　　　0005
Unit
电话　67204381
Tel
车号　京 B-J9458
Taxi No.
证号　023202
Certificate No.
日期　2010-01-02
Date
时间　10:00-10:14
Time
单价　　　2.00
Unit price
里程　　　4.4
Mileage
等候　00:05:48
Wait
状态　　　　1
State
金额　¥15.00
Amount charged
卡号　------
Card No.
卡原额　------
Card original sum
卡余额　------
Card balance sum
密　码
Password

Wǒ quánshēn dōu bù shūfu

我 全身 都 不 舒服

I am not feeling well at all.

听说练习 Listening and Speaking Exercises

1 发音练习。

Pronunciation drills.

Read the ancient poem.

静夜思	Jìng Yè Sī
（唐）李白	(Táng) Lǐ Bái
床前明月光，	Chuáng qián míng yuè guāng,
疑是地上霜。	Yí shì dì shàng shuāng.
举头望明月，	Jǔ tóu wàng míng yuè,
低头思故乡。	Dī tóu sī gù xiāng.

18 **2** 听录音，并回答听到的问题。

2~6

Listen and answer the questions you hear.

1 _____

2 _____

3 _____

4 _____

5 _____

3 听对话，并判断正误。

Listen to the following dialogue and decide whether the statements are true (T) or false (F).

1. 病人是脑子（nǎozi, brain）有病。　（　　）

2. 病人没有发烧。　（　　）

3. 病人嗓子发炎。　（　　）

4. 病人是感冒。　（　　）

4 听录音，并填空。

Listen and fill in the blanks.

1. 我＿＿＿＿＿＿＿＿。

2. 今天＿＿＿＿＿＿＿很冷。

3. 全身不＿＿＿＿＿＿＿。

4. 你看病＿＿＿＿＿＿＿他看病？

5. 你＿＿＿＿＿＿＿不舒服？

5 听录音，写汉字。

Listen and write characters.

6 角色扮演。

Role-play.

Listen to and imitate the dialogue together with your partner. Try to get the meaning of the dialogue with the help of your friends, teachers or dictionaries.

读写练习 Reading and Writing Exercises

1 按正确的笔顺描汉字，并在后边的空格里写汉字。

Trace over the characters, following the correct stroke order. Then copy the characters in the blank spaces.

予	乛マ予予	予	予
母	乚𠮥𠮥母母	母	母
冬	夂夂冬冬冬	冬	冬
令	丿人人今令	令	令
牙	一二于牙	牙	牙
衣	丶一宀才衣衣	衣	衣
自	丿丨自自自自	自	自
发	乚少发发发	发	发
主	丶一二主主	主	主
厂	一厂	厂	厂

2 在空格里写汉字，注意汉字的部件。

Write the characters in the blank spaces, paying attention to the character components.

quán	人 + 王	全
shū	丿 + 丰 + 口 + 予	舒
fú	月 + 卩 + 又	服
měi	𠂉 + 母	每

téng	疒＋冬	疼									
sǎng	口＋ヌ＋ヌ＋ヌ＋木	嗓									
duàn	钅＋段	锻									
liàn	火＋东	炼									
xiǎng	木＋目＋心	想									
bìng	疒＋丙	病									
tǐ	亻＋本	体									
ba	口＋巴	吧									
lěng	冫＋令	冷									
chuān	穴＋牙	穿									
xiū	亻＋木	休									
xī	自＋心	息									
guà	扌＋土＋土	挂									
yán	火＋火	炎									
shāo	火＋戈＋兀	烧									
gǎn	戌＋一＋口＋心	感									
mào	冃＋目	冒									
zhù	亻＋主	住									
yào	艹＋纟＋勺	药									
yuàn	厂＋白＋小＋心	愿									

3 把下列汉字分解成部件。

Divide the following characters into character components.

（1）出　　　　　　　（4）起

（2）画　　　　　　　（5）题

（3）进

4 为下列汉字标注拼音，并在括号里写出笔画数。

Give the *pinyin* of the following characters and write the stroke numbers in the parentheses.

（1）广 ＿＿＿＿＿（　　）　　　（6）目 ＿＿＿＿＿（　　）

　　　厂 ＿＿＿＿＿（　　）　　　　　自 ＿＿＿＿＿（　　）

（2）今 ＿＿＿＿＿（　　）　　　（7）太 ＿＿＿＿＿（　　）

　　　令 ＿＿＿＿＿（　　）　　　　　犬 ＿＿＿＿＿（　　）

（3）全 ＿＿＿（　　）　　　　（8）休 ＿＿＿＿＿（　　）

　　　金 ＿＿＿＿＿（　　）　　　　　体 ＿＿＿＿＿（　　）

（4）几 ＿＿＿＿＿（　　）　　　（9）主 ＿＿＿＿＿（　　）

　　　儿 ＿＿＿＿＿（　　）　　　　　王 ＿＿＿＿＿（　　）

（5）问 ＿＿＿＿＿（　　）　　　（10）作 ＿＿＿＿＿（　　）

　　　间 ＿＿＿＿＿（　　）　　　　　昨 ＿＿＿＿＿（　　）

5 根据所给拼音，在第二行中找到能与第一行汉字组成词语的汉字，并连线。

Find a character in the second line which can be combined with a character in the first line to make a word according to the *pinyin* provided. Draw a line to connect the two.

（1）yīnggāi　　（2）shuìjiào　　（3）shūfu　　（4）duànliàn　　（5）shēntǐ

　　身　　　应　　　睡　　　舒　　　锻

　　服　　　觉　　　体　　　炼　　　该

6 根据所给拼音，用括号里的汉字造句，并译成英文。

Organize the characters in parentheses into Chinese sentences according to the *pinyin* given, and then translate the sentences into English.

（1）Tā quánshēn dōu bù shūfu.
（不都全身他舒服）

_____ 。

_____ .

（2）Mǎ Dàwéi yīnggāi qù yīyuàn kànbìng.
（医院马大为去应该病看）

_____ 。

_____ .

（3）Tā sǎngzi fāyán, yǒudiǎnr fāshāo.
（嗓子发炎有点儿他发烧）

_____ 。

_____ .

（4）Nǐ yuànyì chī zhōngyào ma?
（中药愿意你吃吗）

_____ ?

_____ ?

（5）Sòng Huá gēn tā yìqǐ qù yīyuàn kànbìng.
（跟他一起宋华去医院看病）

_____ 。

_____ .

7 用汉字填表。

Fill in the form with characters.

学生卡

姓　名		性别		国籍	
出生年月日			出生地		

New words：

① 卡　　　kǎ　　　　　N　　　card
② 姓名　　xìngmíng　　N　　　name
③ 性别　　xìngbié　　　N　　　sex
④ 国籍　　guójí　　　　N　　　nationality

8 猜字谜。

Character riddle.

山外有山。

（The key is a character.）

（Key to Exercise 8 in Lesson 11: 回）

9 完成下列对话。

Complete the following dialogues.

（1）A: _____?

　　　B: 我全身都不舒服。

（2）A: _____?

　　　B: 我们现在去医院。

（3）A: _____?

　　　B: 我愿意吃中药。

（4）A: _____?

　　　B: 我头疼。

10 连接Ⅰ和Ⅱ两部分的词语，组成词组。

Make phrases by matching words from part Ⅰ with those from part Ⅱ. Draw a line to connect them.

11 把下列陈述句变成选择问句或是非问句。
Change the following statements into alternative questions or V/A-not-V/A questions.

（1）我要睡觉，不想去看病。→ _____？

（2）今天天气很冷。→ _____？

（3）她不用住院。→ _____？

（4）他愿意吃中药，不愿意吃西药。→ _____？

（5）我每天锻炼身体。→ _____？

12 用所给词语造句。
Make sentences with the words given.

愿意：_____

休息：_____

吧：_____

穿：_____

想：_____

锻炼：_____

13 根据本课课文判断正误。
Decide whether the statements are true (T) or false (F) according to the text of this lesson.

（1）丁力波嗓子疼。 （ ）

（2）马大为星期一去医院。 （ ）

（3）马大为今年三十二岁。 （ ）

（4）马大为是8号。 （ ）

（5）马大为告诉林娜他下午不能去锻炼。 （ ）

14 写一段话描述下列图片。
Write a short paragraph describing the pictures below.

15 判断下列句子的语法是否正确。
Decide whether the statements are grammatically correct (√) or wrong (×).

（1）你吃想不想蛋糕?　　　　　(　　　)

（2）他要不要住院?　　　　　(　　　)

（3）你愿意不愿意吃药?　　　　(　　　)

（4）她愿意吃药还是不愿意住院?　(　　　)

16 读短文，并回答问题。
Read the passage and answer the questions.

马大为的身体

马大为身体很好。天气很冷，他常常穿很少的衣服。昨天下雪（xuě, snow），他只穿衬衫（chènshān, shirt）。今天上午他没有起床。他不能去上课。他说："我头疼。"我说："你应该多穿点儿衣服。"

问题　Questions

（1）马大为身体好吗？

（2）马大为为什么头疼？

（3）马大为为什么不能上课？

17 用学过的汉字描述一次看病的经历。（不少于50个字）

Use the characters you have learned to describe your experience seeing a doctor (more than 50 characters).

Wǒ rènshile yí ge piàoliang de gūniang
我 认识了一个 漂亮 的 姑娘
I knew a beautiful girl.

听说练习 Listening and Speaking Exercises

1 发音练习。

Pronunciation drills.

Read the following Chinese idioms aloud.

① 失败是成功之母。

Shībài shì chénggōng zhī mǔ.

② 一年之计在于春，一日之计在于晨。

Yì nián zhī jì zàiyú chūn, yí rì zhī jì zàiyú chén.

③ 三天打鱼，两天晒网。

Sān tiān dǎ yú, liǎng tiān shài wǎng.

19
2~6

2 听录音，并回答听到的问题。

Listen and answer the questions you hear.

① _____

② _____

③ _____

④ _____

3 听录音，并判断正误。

Listen and decide whether the statements are true (T) or false (F).

① 马大为的女朋友很漂亮。　（　　　）

② 林娜和丁力波在学院认识了小燕子。 （　　）

③ 马大为不想告诉他的朋友他有了女朋友。 （　　）

4 听录音，并填空。
Listen and fill in the blanks.

① 我_____你们吃饭。

② 他们找了_____公司。

③ 我_____了一个漂亮的姑娘。

④ 你去_____了吗？

⑤ 林娜，_____你一件事。

5 听录音，写汉字。
Listen and write characters.

6 角色扮演。
Role-play.

Listen to and imitate the dialogue together with your partner.

7 互动练习：和你的语伴一起谈论学生宿舍。
Interactions: Talk about the students' dormitory together with your partner.

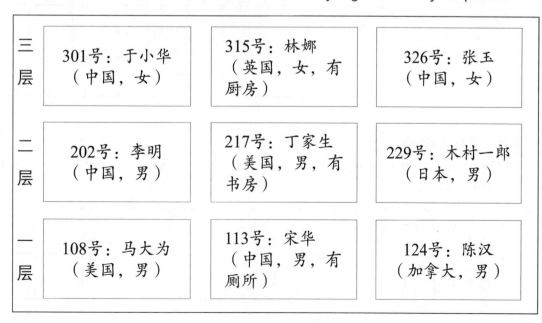

三层	301号：于小华（中国，女）	315号：林娜（英国，女，有厨房）	326号：张玉（中国，女）
二层	202号：李明（中国，男）	217号：丁家生（美国，男，有书房）	229号：木村一郎（日本，男）
一层	108号：马大为（美国，男）	113号：宋华（中国，男，有厕所）	124号：陈汉（加拿大，男）

读写练习 *Reading and Writing Exercises*

1 按正确的笔顺描汉字，并在后边的空格里写汉字。
Trace over the characters, following the correct stroke order. Then copy the characters in the blank spaces.

古	一 十 十 古 古	古	古					
良	、 ラ ヨ 彐 白 良 良	良	良					
斤	^ 丆 斤 斤 斤	斤	斤					
事	一 一 戸 戸 写 写 写 事	事	事					
步	丨 ト ヰ 止 虍 步 步	步	步					
电	丨 冂 冂 日 电	电	电					
户	、 ラ 彐 户	户	户					
方	、 亠 宁 方	方	方					
豆	一 冖 冂 丏 戸 豆 豆	豆	豆					
办	乛 力 办 办	办	办					
竹	丿 ト 丿 伫 竹 竹	竹	竹					
反	一 厂 反 反	反	反					

2 在空格里写汉字，注意汉字的部件。
Write the characters in the blank spaces, paying attention to the character components.

| gū | 女 + 古 | 姑 | | | | | |
| niáng | 女 + 良 | 娘 | | | | | |

tīng	口 + 斤	听							
dé	彳 + 日 + 一 + 寸	得							
gào	丷 + 口	告							
sù	讠 + 斤	诉							
jiàn	亻 + 牛	件							
sàn	廿 + 月 + 攵	散							
yǐng	日 + 京 + 彡	影							
kā	口 + 力 + 口	咖							
fēi	口 + 非	啡							
sù	宀 + 亻 + 百	宿							
shè	人 + 舌	舍							
fáng	户 + 方	房							
zū	禾 + 且	租							
chú	厂 + 豆 + 寸	厨							
cè	厂 + 贝 + 刂	厕							
suǒ	户 + 斤	所							
gōng	八 + 厶	公							
dǎ	扌 + 丁	打							

huà	讠 + 舌	话							
ràng	讠 + 上	让							
bāng	韦 + 阝 + 巾	帮							
zhù	且 + 力	助							
wèi	口 + 田 + 衣	喂							
wèi	亻 + 立	位							
jīng	纟 + 圣	经							
lǐ	王 + 里	理							
děng	竹 + 士 + 寸	等							
fàn	饣 + 反	饭							

3 为下列汉字标注拼音，并把每一组汉字相同的部首写在括号里。

Give the *pinyin* of the following characters and write the radical common to the characters in each group in the parenthesis.

（1）妈　姐　妹　好　姑　娘　她　娜　　　（　　）

（2）他　你　们　做　件　什　休　体　作

　　　化　住　位　候　　　　　　　　　　（　　）

（3）语　请　谁　谢　让　认　识　说　话

　　　诉　课　该　　　　　　　　　　　　（　　）

（4）吗　吧　叫　吃　喝　号　只　哪　告

　　　呢　嗓　喂　啊　咖　啡　可　听　　（　　）

（5）这　进　还　送　　　　　　　　　　　（　　）

4 选择恰当的汉字填空。
Fill in the blanks with the proper characters.

（1）你身_____怎么样？

    A.休   B.体   C.本

（2）我告_____你一件事儿。

    A.听   B.所   C.诉

（3）马大为_____身都不舒服。

    A.金   B.全   C.会

（4）你愿_____吃中药吗？

    A.思   B.想   C.意

5 朗读并写汉字。
Read and copy the following characters indicating numbers.

读音 Pronunciation	yī	èr	sān	sì	wǔ	liù	qī	bā	jiǔ	shí
小写 Ordinary form	一	二	三	四	五	六	七	八	九	十
大写 Capital form	壹	贰	叁	肆	伍	陆	柒	捌	玖	拾
描写 Trace	壹	贰	叁	肆	伍	陆	柒	捌	玖	拾
临写 Copy										

6 根据所给拼音，用括号里的汉字组成句子，并译成英文。
Organize the characters in parentheses into Chinese sentences according to the *pinyin* given and then translate the sentences into English.

（1）Mǎ Dàwéi qǐng zū fáng gōngsī bāngzhù tā zhǎo fángzi.

    （马大为请房租帮助公司找他房子）

    _____。

    _____.

（2）Sòng Huá ràng nǐ gěi tā dǎ diànhuà.
（让打他宋华电话你给）

_____ 。

_____ .

（3）Tā déle gǎnmào, sǎngzi fāyán.
（嗓子发炎他感冒得了）

_____ 。

_____ .

（4）Tāmen qù kànle yí tào yǒu chúfáng hé cèsuǒ de fángzi.
（有厨房和厕所的房子去他们一套看了）

_____ 。

_____ .

（5）Xīngqīliù wǎnshang qī diǎn, tā qǐng nǚ péngyou kàn diànyǐng.
（晚上七点星期六女朋友请他看电影）

_____ 。

_____ .

7 模仿例子写便条。

Follow the example to write a note.

Example:

陈老师：
　　我今天头疼，还有点儿发烧，很不舒服。医生说应该休息两天。对不起，我明天不能来上课。
　　　　　　　马大为
　　　　　　十一月二十八日

You visited a friend, but he was not in. Write a note to him.

8 猜字谜。

Character riddle.

太少了一点儿。

（The key is a character.）

（Key to Exercise 8 in Lesson 12: 出）

9 完成下列对话。

Complete the following dialogues.

（1）A: _____?

　　 B: 我当然想租房子。

（2）A: _____?

　　 B: 我吃了药。

（3）A: _____?

　　 B: 我请了他们。

（4）A: _____?

　　 B: 我给他打了一个电话。

10 连接Ⅰ和Ⅱ两部分的词语，组成词组。

Make phrases by matching words from part Ⅰ with those from part Ⅱ. Draw a line to connect them.

Ⅰ
请
租
打
有
找

Ⅱ
电话
吃饭
房子
人
朋友

11 把下列陈述句变成是非问句，并给出否定回答。

Change the following statements into V/A-not-V/A questions, and then give the negative answers to the questions.

（1）我上午给他打了电话。

→ _____?

_____。

（2）我们看了一套房子。

→ _____?

_____。

（3）我昨天请他吃了饭。

→ _____?

_____。

（4）他星期六找了经理。

→ _____?

_____。

（5）他买了一斤苹果。

→ _____?

_____。

12 用所给词语造句。

Make sentences with the words given.

听说：_____

了：_____

让： _____

办： _____

可能： _____

等： _____

13 根据本课课文判断正误。

Decide whether the statements are true (T) or false (F) according to the text of this lesson.

（1）马大为认识了一个男朋友。 （ ）

（2）马大为想租房子。 （ ）

（3）宋华看的那间房子很贵。 （ ）

（4）丁力波想租房子。 （ ）

（5）宋华星期天和马大为一起去租房子。 （ ）

14 写一段话描述下列图片。

Write a short paragraph describing the picture below.

15 判断下列句子的语法是否正确。

Decide whether the statements are grammatically correct (√) or wrong (×).

(1) 我让不她来。　　　　　　　　(　　)

(2) 这两天太忙我。　　　　　　　(　　)

(3) 她让我等她。　　　　　　　　(　　)

(4) 我给我妈妈打了一个电话。　(　　)

16 读短文，并回答问题。

Read the passage and answer the questions.

在新家

马大为租了一套房子，他非常高兴。他请他的中国朋友来吃饭。他的房子里有卧室、客厅、厨房和厕所。他的房子很好，可是现在没有家具（jiājù, furniture）。朋友们都坐在地上。

问题　Questions

(1) 马大为的新家怎么样?

(2) 朋友们为什么坐在地上?

(3) 马大为请中国朋友来新家做什么?

17 用学过的汉字描述你的宿舍或你家。（不少于50个字）

Use the characters you have learned to describe your dormitory or your home (more than 50 characters).

A Summary of the Optative Verbs

The optative verbs studied so far are:

intention	想 不想 想不想	要 不想 要不要	愿意 不愿意 愿意不愿意
necessity		要 不用 要不要	应该 不应该 应该不应该
permission		能 不能 能不能	可以 不可以 可以不可以
ability	会 不会 会不会	能 不能 能不能	可以 不能 可以不可以
possibility	会 不会 会不会		可能 不可能 可能不可能

Zhù nǐ Shèngdàn kuàilè

祝你 圣诞 快乐

Merry Christmas to you!

（复习 Review）

 听说练习 *Listening and Speaking Exercises*

1 发音练习。

Pronunciation drills.

Read the following words, phrases, or sentences aloud, paying special attention to the third-tone sandhi and word stress of polysyllabic words.

葡萄酒	星期天	脏衣服	念生词	去邮局
爸爸妈妈	你们宿舍	留学生楼	中国朋友	中文名字
学习汉语	语法问题	复习课文	练习口语	圣诞礼物

我很好。

你也很好。

马雨小姐也想买本子。

我给你买两斤苹果。

2 听录音，并回答听到的问题。

20
2~6

Listen and answer the questions you hear.

1 _____

2 _____

3 _____

4 _____

5 _____

3 听对话，并判断正误。

Listen to the following dialogue and decide whether the statements are true (T) or false (F).

① 丁力波的外婆家在中国。　　　（　　）

② 林娜的外婆家在北京。　　　　（　　）

③ 他们去丁力波家打球。　　　　（　　）

④ 丁力波请大家去吃火鸡（huǒjī, turkey）。（　　）

4 听录音，并填空。

Listen and fill in the blanks.

① 我给你打＿＿＿＿＿＿＿。

② 他们都喜欢＿＿＿＿＿＿。

③ 请等＿＿＿＿＿＿。

④ 祝你圣诞＿＿＿＿＿＿！

5 听录音，写汉字。

Listen and write characters.

6 角色扮演。

Role-play.

Listen to and imitate the dialogue together with your partner. Try to get the meaning of the dialogue with the help of your friends, teachers or dictionaries.

 读写练习　Reading and Writing Exercises

1 按正确的笔顺描汉字，并在后边的空格里写汉字。
Trace over the characters, following the correct stroke order. Then copy the characters in the blank spaces.

才	一 十 才	才	才						
由	丨 冂 冂 由 由	由	由						
州	丶 丿 丬 州 州 州	州	州						

2 在空格里写汉字，注意汉字的部件。
Write the characters in the blank spaces, paying attention to the character components.

shèng	又 + 土	圣							
dàn	讠 + 正 + 乂	诞							
gāng	冈 + 刂	刚							
yóu	由 + 阝	邮							
jú	尸 + 可	局							
jì	宀 + 大 + 可	寄							
sǎo	扌 + 彐	扫							
zāng	月 + 广 + 土	脏							
xǐ	氵 + 先	洗							
pó	氵 + 皮 + 女	婆							
nán	十 + 冂 + 羊	南							

lǚ	方 + ⌐ + 氏	旅							
xíng	彳 + 亍	行							
liú	𠃌 + 刀 + 田	留							
niàn	今 + 心	念							
cí	讠 + 司	词							
fù	⌐ + 日 + 夂	复							
liàn	纟 + 东	练							
fǎ	氵 + 去	法							
jié	艹 + 卩	节							
lǐ	礻 + 乚	礼							
wù	牛 + 勿	物							
ōu	区 + 欠	欧							
zhōu	氵 + 州	洲							
hǎi	氵 + 每	海							

3 为下列汉字标注拼音，并把每一组汉字相同的部首写在括号里。

Give the *pinyin* of the following characters and write the radicals common to the characters in each group in the parentheses.

（1） 提　　打　　找　　扫　　挂　　授　　报　（　　）

（2） 您　　想　　意　　思　　愿　　怎　　念

　　　感　　　　　　　　　　　　　　　　　　（　　）

（3） 绍　　红　　经　　给　　练　　　　　　　（　　）

（4）友　　发　　圣　　对　　欢　　　　　　　　（　　）

（5）汉　　酒　　法　　游　　泳　　没　　海

　　　洲　　洗　　漂　　波　　　　　　　　　　（　　）

（6）节　　英　　苹　　药　　蕉　　葡　　萄（　　）

（7）会　　舍　　全　　金　　今　　拿　　　　（　　）

（8）时　　明　　昨　　晚　　星　　是　　　　（　　）

4 为下列每组汉字和词语标注拼音，并译成英文。
Give the *pinyin* for the following groups of characters and words and then translate them into English.

（1）学

　　学习　　　　　　　　　　学院

　　学生　　　　　　　　　　大学

（2）语

　　汉语　　　　　　　　　　英语

　　外语　　　　　　　　　　语法

（3）国

　　中国　　　　　　　　　　英国

　　美国　　　　　　　　　　外国

（4）方

　　南方　　　　　　　　　　东方

　　北方　　　　　　　　　　西方

5 选择恰当的汉字填空。
Fill in the blanks with the proper characters.

（1）我给你们＿＿＿＿＿＿绍一下儿。

　　A. 个　　　　B. 介　　　　C. 竹

（2）你认_____陈老师吗?

    A. 只   B. 时   C. 识

（3）马大为_____语言学院学习汉语。

    A. 在   B. 再   C. 住

（4）他很喜欢锻_____身体。

    A. 练   B. 炼   C. 陈

6 根据所给拼音，用括号里的汉字组成句子，并译成英文。

Organize the characters in parentheses into Chinese sentences according to the *pinyin* given and then translate the sentences into English.

（1）Dīng Lìbō shēntǐ zěnmeyàng?

    （丁力波怎么样身体）

    _____?

    _____?

（2）Lín Nà de sùshè hěn piàoliang.

    （宿舍林娜的漂亮很）

    _____。

    _____.

（3）Xīngqīliù xiàwǔ wǒmen qù kànle yí ge Měiguó diànyǐng.

    （看了电影一个美国去我们星期六下午）

    _____。

    _____.

（4）Tā qù yóujú gěi dìdi、 mèimei jì Shèngdàn lǐwù.

    （去邮局他寄圣诞给弟弟妹妹礼物）

    _____。

    _____.

（5）Wǒ zhù péngyoumen Shèngdàn kuàilè.

    （祝朋友们我圣诞快乐）

    _____。

    _____.

7 模仿例子，用汉字写圣诞卡。

Imitating the example, write a Christmas card in Chinese.

Example: a greeting card written by Ding Libo.

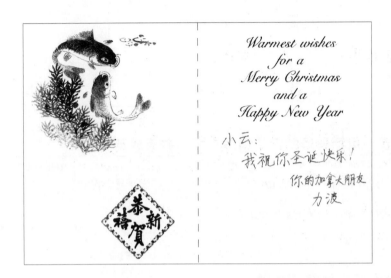

(Key to Exercise 8 in Lesson 13: 大)

8 完成下列对话。

Complete the following dialogues.

（1）A: _____?

　　 B: 我很喜欢在中国过圣诞节。

（2）A: _____?

　　 B: 我能帮你买票。

（3）A: _____?

　　 B: 我在北京过圣诞节。

（4）A: _____?

　　 B: 他圣诞节去上海旅游。

9 连接 I 和 II 两部分的词语，组成词组。
Make phrases by matching words from part I with those from part II. Draw a line to connect them.

10 把下列陈述句变成是非问句。
Change the following statements into V/A-not-V/A questions.

（1）他给妈妈寄了圣诞礼物。→ _____?

（2）我不去参加聚会。→ _____?

（3）你应该在北京买礼物。→ _____?

（4）他们去南方旅行。→ _____?

（5）我不能去旅行。→ _____?

11 用所给词语造句。
Make sentences with the words given.

不好意思：_____

礼物：_____

寄：_____

祝：_____

住：_____

刚才：＿＿＿＿＿＿＿＿＿＿＿＿＿＿＿＿＿＿＿＿

脏：＿＿＿＿＿＿＿＿＿＿＿＿＿＿＿＿＿＿＿＿

12　根据本课课文判断正误。

Decide whether the statements are true (T) or false (F) according to the text of this lesson.

（1）留学生一个人一个房间。　　　　　　　（　　　）

（2）上海很漂亮。　　　　　　　　　　　　（　　　）

（3）圣诞节丁力波的妈妈和爸爸去欧洲旅行。（　　　）

（4）丁力波在上海过圣诞节。　　　　　　　（　　　）

（5）丁力波不在北京过圣诞节。　　　　　　（　　　）

13　写一段话描述下列图片。
Write a short paragraph describing the pictures below.

14 判断下列句子的语法是否正确。

Decide whether the statements are grammatically correct (√) or wrong (✕).

（1）她没有了吃。 （   ）

（2）我还常常问他们语法的问题。 （   ）

（3）他打工了在北京。 （   ）

（4）我刚才去了邮局。 （   ）

15 读短文，并回答问题。

Read the passage and answer the questions.

节 日

中国有很多节日，最（zuì, the most）重要（zhòngyào, important）、最热闹（rènao, bustling）的节日是春节。

现在，在中国的外国人很多，不少外国人都过圣诞节。一些中国的年轻人也过圣诞节。他们互相祝贺圣诞快乐。圣诞节的晚上，北京到处是圣诞音乐、圣诞礼物和圣诞聚会。圣诞节进入了中国、进入了北京。

问题 Questions

（1）中国人都过圣诞节吗？

（2）圣诞节的晚上北京到处是什么？

（3）中国最重要的节日是什么？

16 用学过的汉字描述你们国家的一个节日。 （不少于50个字）

Use the characters you have learned to describe a festival in your country (more than 50 characters).

17 阅读下面的广告，并找出：
Read the following advertisement and find out:

a. The amount one needs to pay for the tour: _____

b. The telephone number if one wants to call the travel agency in the evening:

_____

c. How many days the tour lasts: _____

d. Can you figure out any other information?

_____

_____

The Structural Particle "的" in Attributes

In what case is the structural particle "的" needed between the attribute and the central word it modifies? The following rules summarize the uses of this particle studied in the previous lessons:

(1) When a noun functions as an attribute to express possession, "的" is usually needed. For example: "张教授的名片", "妈妈的电话", "外语系的学生". When a noun functions as an attribute to indicate the qualities or attributes of the central word, "的" is usually not used. For example: "中国人", "汉语学院", "生日蛋糕".

(2) When a personal pronoun functions as an attribute to express possession, "的" is usually needed. For example: "我的书", "你的照片", "他的名字". If the central word modified by the personal pronoun denotes a relative or a work unit, "的" is not necessary. For example: "我爸爸", "你们家", "他们学院".

(3) When a numeral-measure word（or a demonstrative pronoun plus a measure word）functions as an attribute, "的" is never used. For example: "三十五个学生", "两斤苹果", "这间房子".

(4) If a monosyllabic adjective functions as an attribute, "的" is not needed. For example: "男朋友", "小狗", "红酒". If an attribute is a disyllabic adjective, "的" must be used after it. For example: "有名的音乐", "可爱的贝贝".

(5) When a verb, verbal phrase, or subject-predicate phrase functions as an attribute, "的" is required. For example: "来的人", "有厨房的房子", "你住的宿舍".